2013 Conference of the North American Chapter of the Association for Computation Linguistics: Human Language Technologies (NAACL HLT 2013)

Demonstration Session

Atlanta, Georgia, USA
10-12 June 2013

ISBN: 978-1-62748-840-2

Printed from e-media with permission by:

Curran Associates, Inc.
57 Morehouse Lane
Red Hook, NY 12571

CURRAN ASSOCIATES INC. proceedings.com

Some format issues inherent in the e-media version may also appear in this print version.

Printed by Curran Associates, Inc. (2013)

Association for Computational Linguistics
209 N. Eighth Street
Stroudsburg, Pennsylvania 18360

Phone: 1-570-476-8006
Fax: 1-570-476-0860

acl@aclweb.org

Additional copies of this publication are available from:

Curran Associates, Inc.
57 Morehouse Lane
Red Hook, NY 12571 USA
Phone: 845-758-0400
Fax: 845-758-2634
Email: curran@proceedings.com
Web: www.proceedings.com

Table of Contents

Conference Program

Monday, June 10, 2013

18:30–20:30 Poster and Demonstrations Session

DALE: A Word Sense Disambiguation System for Biomedical Documents Trained using Automatically Labeled Examples
Judita Preiss and Mark Stevenson

Topic Models and Metadata for Visualizing Text Corpora
Justin Snyder, Rebecca Knowles, Mark Dredze, Matthew Gormley and Travis Wolfe

TMTprime: A Recommender System for MT and TM Integration
Aswarth Abhilash Dara, Sandipan Dandapat, Declan Groves and Josef van Genabith

Anafora: A Web-based General Purpose Annotation Tool
Wei-Te Chen and Will Styler

A Web Application for the Diagnostic Evaluation of Machine Translation over Specific Linguistic Phenomena
Antonio Toral, Sudip Kumar Naskar, Joris Vreeke, Federico Gaspari and Declan Groves

KooSHO: Japanese Text Input Environment based on Aerial Hand Writing
Masato Hagiwara and Soh Masuko

UMLS::Similarity: Measuring the Relatedness and Similarity of Biomedical Concepts
Bridget McInnes, Ted Pedersen, Serguei Pakhomov, Ying Liu and Genevieve Melton-Meaux

KELVIN: a tool for automated knowledge base construction
Paul McNamee, James Mayfield, Tim Finin, Tim Oates, Dawn Lawrie, Tan Xu and Douglas Oard

Argviz: Interactive Visualization of Topic Dynamics in Multi-party Conversations
Viet-An Nguyen, Yuening Hu, Jordan Boyd-Graber and Philip Resnik

DALE: A Word Sense Disambiguation System for Biomedical Documents Trained using Automatically Labeled Examples

Judita Preiss and **Mark Stevenson**
Department of Computer Science, University of Sheffield
Regent Court, 211 Portobello
Sheffield S1 4DP, United Kingdom
j.preiss,m.stevenson@dcs.shef.ac.uk

Abstract

Automatic interpretation of documents is hampered by the fact that language contains terms which have multiple meanings. These ambiguities can still be found when language is restricted to a particular domain, such as biomedicine. Word Sense Disambiguation (WSD) systems attempt to resolve these ambiguities but are often only able to identify the meanings for a small set of ambiguous terms. DALE (Disambiguation using Automatically Labeled Examples) is a supervised WSD system that can disambiguate a wide range of ambiguities found in biomedical documents. DALE uses the UMLS Metathesaurus as both a sense inventory and as a source of information for automatically generating labeled training examples. DALE is able to disambiguate biomedical documents with the coverage of unsupervised approaches and accuracy of supervised methods.

1 Introduction

Word Sense Disambiguation (WSD) is an important challenge for any automatic text processing system since language contains ambiguous terms which can be difficult to interpret. Ambiguous terms that are found in biomedical documents include words, phrases and abbreviations (Schuemie et al., 2005). Identifying the correct interpretation of ambiguous terms is important to ensure that the text can be processed appropriately.

Many WSD systems developed for biomedical documents are based on supervised learning, for example (McInnes et al., 2007; Martinez and Baldwin, 2011); these have the advantage of being more accurate than unsupervised approaches. However, WSD systems based on supervised learning rely on manually labeled examples consisting of instances of an ambiguous term marked with their correct interpretations. Manually labeled examples are very expensive to create and are consequently only available for a few hundred terms, with each new domain (with its specialist vocabulary) needing new examples labeled. The majority of supervised WSD systems are limited to resolving a small number of ambiguous terms and, despite their accuracy, are not suitable for use within applications.

An alternative approach is to use *automatically labeled examples* which can be generated without manual annotation (Leacock et al., 1998). These have been used to generate an all-words WSD system that assigns senses from WordNet (Zhong and Ng, 2010). For biomedical documents the UMLS Metathesaurus (Humphreys et al., 1998b) is a more suitable lexical resource than WordNet and techniques have been developed to create automatically labeled examples for this resource (Stevenson and Guo, 2010). However, to date, automatically labeled examples have only been used as substitutes for ambiguous terms for which manually labeled examples are not available, rather than using them to create a WSD system that can resolve a wider range of ambiguities in biomedical documents.

DALE (Disambiguation using Automatically Labeled Examples) is an online WSD system for biomedical documents that was developed by creating automatically labeled examples for all ambiguous terms in the UMLS Metathesaurus. DALE is able to identify a meaning for any term that is ambiguous in the Metathesaurus and therefore has far greater coverage of ambiguous terms than other supervised WSD systems. Other all-words WSD systems for biomedical documents are unsupervised and do not have as high accuracy as supervised approaches, e.g. (McInnes, 2008; Agirre et al., 2010). An unsupervised WSD algorithm (Humphreys et al., 1998a) is included in MetaMap (Aronson and Lang, 2010) but is unable to resolve all types of sense distinction.

2 The DALE System

2.1 Automatically Labeling Examples

DALE assigns Concept Unique Identifiers (CUIs) from the UMLS Metathesaurus. The WSD algorithm in DALE is based around a supervised algorithm (Stevenson et al., 2008) trained using automatically labeled examples. The examples are generated using two methods: *Monosemous relatives* and *Co-occurring concepts* (Stevenson and Guo, 2010). Both approaches take a single CUI, c, as input and use information from the UMLS Metathesaurus to search Medline and identify instances of c that can be used as labeled examples. The difference between the two approaches is that they make use of different information from the Metathesaurus.

Both approaches are provided with a set of ambiguous CUIs from the UMLS Metathesaurus, which represent the possible meanings of an ambiguous term, and a target number of training examples to be generated for each CUI. The UMLS Metathesaurus contains a number of data files which are exploited within these techniques, including: 1. `AMBIGLUI`: a list of cases where a LUI, a particular lexical variant of a term, is linked to multiple CUIs; 2. `MRCON`: list of all strings and concept names in the Metathesaurus; 3. `MRCOC`: co-occurring concepts.

For the monosemous relatives approach, the strings of monosemous LUIs of the target CUI and its relatives are used to search Medline to retrieve training examples. The monosemous LUIs related to a CUI are defined as any LUIs associated with the CUI in `MRCON` table and not listed in `AMBIGLUI` table. For example, one of the LUIs associated with CUI "C0028707" is L0875433 "Nutrition Science" in `MRCON` table. It is not listed in `AMBIGLUI` table and therefore considered to be a monosemous LUI of CUI "C0028707". The string "Nutrition Science" can be used to identify examples of CUI "C0028707".

The co-occurring concept approach works differently: instead of using strings of monosemous LUIs of the target CUI and its relatives, the strings associated with LUIs of a number of co-occurring CUIs of the target CUI and its relatives found in MRCOC table are used. For instance, "C0025520", "C1524024" and "C0079107" are the top three co-occurring CUIs of CUI "C0015677" in `MRCOC` table. The strings associated with LUIs of these three CUIs can be used to retrieve examples of CUI "C0015677" by searching for abstracts containing all the LUIs of the co-occurring CUIs.

These approaches were used to create labeled examples for ambiguous CUIs in the 2010AB, 2011AA, 2011AB and 2012AA versions of the UMLS Metathesaurus. Examples could be generated for 95.2%, 96.2%, 96.2% and 98% of the CUIs in each version of the Metathesaurus respectively. Neither technique was able to generate examples for the remaining CUIs, however none of these CUIs appear in the corresponding MetaMapped version of the Medline Baseline Repository (`http://mbr.nlm.nih.gov`), suggesting these CUIs do not tend to be mentioned within documents. 100 examples were generated for each CUI since using an equal number of examples for each CUI produces the best WSD performance in the absence of other information about the likelihood of each CUI (Cheng et al., 2012).

The labeled examples are converted into feature vectors consisting of lemmas of all content words in the same sentence as the ambiguous word and, in addition, the lemmas of all content words in a ± 4-word window around it. A single feature vector is created for each CUI by taking the centroid of the feature vectors created from the labeled examples of that CUI. These vectors are stored in the Centroid Database for later use.

2.2 Word Sense Disambiguation

WSD of an ambiguous term is carried out by compiling a list of all its possible CUIs and comparing their centroids against a feature vector created from

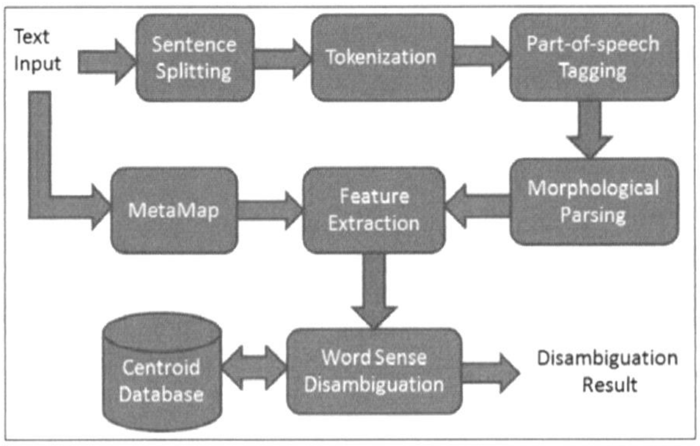

Figure 1: DALE system diagram showing the stages in the WSD process

the sentence containing the ambiguous term. Processing is carried out in multiple stages (see Fig. 1). MetaMap (Aronson and Lang, 2010) is applied to the text to identify ambiguous terms (identifying terms includes some level of multiword detection) and their possible CUIs (UMLS lookup of the identified terms). The input text is also fed into a pipeline to carry out sentence splitting, tokenization, part-of-speech tagging and morphological analysis. Information added by this pipeline is used to create a feature vector for each ambiguous term identified by MetaMap. Finally, the Word Sense Disambiguation module uses cosine similarity to compare the centroid of each possible CUI of the ambiguous term (retrieved from the Centroid Database) with the ambiguous term's feature vector (Stevenson et al., 2008). The most similar CUI is selected for each ambiguous term.

2.3 Online System

DALE is available as a web service with multiple interfaces:

The *Interactive interface* enables a user to submit a piece of text to the system and view the result in an intuitive way. Terms in the result are marked according to their polysemy: blue denotes that it has only one meaning in Metathesaurus (i.e. is not ambiguous) while green means that it has multiple meanings. Rolling the mouse over the highlighted items provides access to additional information in a tooltip style window, including the set of possible CUIs and their preferred names. Clicking on one of these CUIs links to the appropriate page from the UMLS Terminology Services (`http://uts.nlm.nih.gov/`). The CUI chosen by the WSD process is shown underlined at the bottom of the window. The result is also available in XML format which can be downloaded by clicking a link in the result page.

The *Batch interface* is more suitable for disambiguating large amounts of texts. A user can upload plain text files to be processed by DALE using the batch interface. The results will be sent to user's email address in XML format as soon as the system finishes processing the file. This interface is supported by a *Job management interface*. A job is created every time a user uploads a file and each job assigned the status of being either "Waiting" or "Running". The user is also emailed a pin code allowing them to access this interface to check the status of their jobs and cancel any waiting jobs.

3 Conclusion

This paper describes DALE, a WSD system for the biomedical domain based on automatically labeled examples. The system is able to disambiguate all ambiguous terms found in the UMLS Metathesaurus. A freely accessible web service is available and offers a set of easy to use interfaces. We intend to update DALE with new versions of the UMLS Metathesaurus as they become available.

The DALE system is available at `http://kta.rcweb.dcs.shef.ac.uk/dale/`

Acknowledgments

The authors are grateful to Weiwei Cheng for his work on the development of the original version of the DALE system. The development of DALE was funded by the UK Engineering and Physical Sciences Research Council (grants EP/H500170/1 and EP/J008427/1) and by a Google Research Award. We would also like to thank the three reviewers whose feedback has improved the clarity of this paper.

References

E. Agirre, A. Sora, and M. Stevenson. 2010. Graph-based word sense disambiguation of biomedical documents. *Bioinformatics*, 26(22):2889–2896.

A. Aronson and F. Lang. 2010. An overview of MetaMap: historical perspective and recent ad-

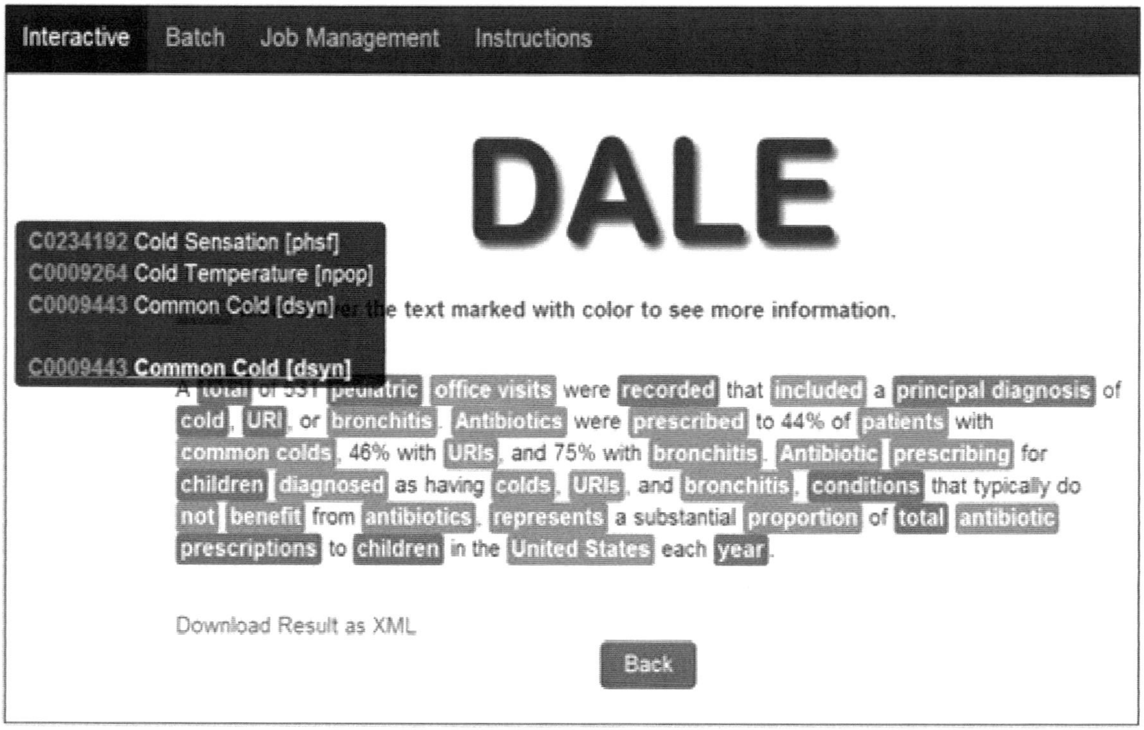

Figure 2: Disambiguation results shown in DALE's Interactive Interface with the ambiguous term 'cold' selected. DALE shows the three possible CUIs for 'cold' identified by MetaMap with the selected CUI (C0009443) highlighted

vances. *Journal of the American Medical Association*, 17(3):229–236.

W. Cheng, J. Preiss, and M. Stevenson. 2012. Scaling up WSD with Automatically Generated Examples. In *BioNLP: Proceedings of the 2012 Workshop on Biomedical Natural Language Processing*, pages 231–239, Montréal, Canada.

K. Humphreys, R. Gaizauskas, S. Azzam, C. Huyck, B. Mitchell, H. Cunningham, and Y. Wilks. 1998a. Description of the LaSIE-II System used in MUC-7. In *Proceedings of the Seventh Message Understanding Conference (MUC-7)*.

L. Humphreys, D. Lindberg, H. Schoolman, and G. Barnett. 1998b. The Unified Medical Language System: An Informatics Research Collaboration. *Journal of the American Medical Informatics Association*, 1(5):1–11.

C. Leacock, M. Chodorow, and G. Miller. 1998. Using Corpus Statistics and WordNet Relations for Sense Identification. *Computational Linguistics*, 24(1):147–165.

D. Martinez and T. Baldwin. 2011. Word sense disambiguation for event trigger word detection in biomedicine. *BMC Bioinformatics*, 12(Suppl 2):S4.

B. McInnes, T. Pedersen, and J. Carlis. 2007. Using UMLS Concept Unique Identifiers (CUIs) for Word Sense Disambiguation in the Biomedical Domain. In *Proceedings of the Annual Symposium of the American Medical Informatics Association*, pages 533–537, Chicago, IL.

Bridget McInnes. 2008. An unsupervised vector approach to biomedical term disambiguation: Integrating UMLS and Medline. In *Proceedings of the ACL-08: HLT Student Research Workshop*, pages 49–54, Columbus, Ohio, June. Association for Computational Linguistics.

M. Schuemie, J. Kors, and B. Mons. 2005. Word Sense Disambiguation in the Biomedical Domain. *Journal of Computational Biology*, 12, 5:554–565.

M. Stevenson and Y. Guo. 2010. Disambiguation of Ambiguous Biomedical Terms using Examples Generated from the UMLS Metathesaurus. *Journal of Biomedical Informatics*, 43(5):762–773.

M. Stevenson, Y. Guo, R. Gaizauskas, and D. Martinez. 2008. Disambiguation of biomedical text using diverse sources of information. *BMC Bioinformatics*, 9(Suppl 11):S7.

Z. Zhong and H. Ng. 2010. It makes sense: A wide-coverage word sense disambiguation system for free text. In *Proceedings of the ACL 2010 System Demonstrations*, pages 78–83, Uppsala, Sweden.

Topic Models and Metadata for Visualizing Text Corpora

Justin Snyder, Rebecca Knowles, Mark Dredze, Matthew R. Gormley, Travis Wolfe
Human Language Technology Center of Excellence
Johns Hopkins University
Baltimore, MD 21211
{jsnyde32,mdredze,mgormley,twolfe3}@jhu.edu, rknowles@haverford.edu

Abstract

Effectively exploring and analyzing large text corpora requires visualizations that provide a high level summary. Past work has relied on faceted browsing of document metadata or on natural language processing of document text. In this paper, we present a new web-based tool that integrates topics learned from an unsupervised topic model in a faceted browsing experience. The user can manage topics, filter documents by topic and summarize views with metadata and topic graphs. We report a user study of the usefulness of topics in our tool.

1 Introduction

When analyzing text corpora, such as newspaper articles, research papers, or historical archives, users need an intuitive way to understand and summarize numerous documents. Exploratory search (Marchionini, 2006) is critical for large corpora that can easily overwhelm users. Corpus visualization tools can provide a high-level view of the data and help direct subsequent exploration. Broadly speaking, such systems can be divided into two groups: those that rely on structured metadata, and those that use information derived from document content.

Metadata Approaches based on metadata include visualizing document metadata alongside a domain ontology (Seeling and Becks, 2003), providing tools to select passages based on annotated words (Correll et al., 2011), and using images and metadata for visualizing related documents (Cataldi et al., 2011).

A natural solution for exploring via metadata is faceted browsing (English et al., 2002; Hearst, 2006; Smith et al., 2006; Yee et al., 2003), a paradigm for filtering commonly used in e-commerce stores. This consists of filtering based on metadata like "brand" or "size", which helps summarize the content of the current document set (Käki, 2005). Studies have shown improved user experiences by facilitating user interactions through facets (Oren et al., 2006) and faceted browsing has been used for aiding search (Fujimura et al., 2006) and exploration (Collins et al., 2009) of text corpora.

However, facets require existing structured metadata fields, which may be limited or unavailable. An alternative is to use NLP to show document content.

Content Topic modeling (Blei et al., 2003), has become very popular for corpus and document understanding. Recent research has focused on aspects highlighted by the topic model, such as topic distributions across the corpus, topic distributions across documents, related topics and words that make up each topic (Chaney and Blei, 2012; Eisenstein et al., 2012), or document relations through topic compositions (Chuang et al., 2012; Gardner et al., 2010).

Newer work has begun to visualize documents in the context of their topics and their metadata, such as topics incorporated with keywords and events (Cui et al., 2011). Other examples include displaying topic prevalence over time (Liu et al., 2009) or helping users understand how real events shape textual trends (Dou et al., 2011). While interfaces may be customized for specific metadata types, e.g. the topical map of National Institutes of Health funding agencies (Talley et al., 2011), these interfaces do not incorporate arbitrary metadata.

2 Combining Metadata and Topics

We present MetaToMATo (Metadata and Topic Model Analysis Toolkit), a visualization tool that combines both metadata and topic models in a single faceted browsing paradigm for exploration and analysis of document collections. While previous work has shown the value of metadata facets, we show that topic model output complements metadata. Providing both in a single interface yields a flexible tool.

We illustrate MetaToMATo with an example adapted from our user study. Consider Sarah, a hypothetical intern in the New York Times archive room who is presented with the following task.

> Your boss explains that although the New York Times metadata fields are fairly comprehensive, sometimes human error leads to oversights or missing entries. Today you've been asked to keep an eye out for documents that mention the New York Marathon but do not include descriptors linking them to that event.

This is corpus exploration: a user is asked to discover relevant information by exploring the corpus. We illustrate the tool with a walk-through.

Corpus Selection The corpus selection page (tool home page) provides information about all available corpora, and allows for corpora upload and deletion.

Sarah selects the New York Times corpus.

Corpus Overview After selecting a corpus, the user sees the corpus overview and configuration page. Across four tabs, the user is presented with more detailed corpus statistics and can customize her visualization experience. The first tab shows general corpus information. The second allows for editing the inferred type (date, quantity, or string) for each metadata attribute to change filtering behavior, hide unhelpful attributes, and choose which attributes to "quick display" in the document collapsed view. On the remaining two tabs, the user can customize date display formats and manage tags.

She selects attributes "Date" and "Byline" for quick display, hides "Series Name", and formats "Date" to show only the date (no times).

Topics View Each topic is displayed in a box containing its name (initially set to its top 3 words) and a list of the top 10 words. Top words within a topic are words with the highest probability of appearing in the corpus. Each topic word is highlighted to show a normalized probability of that word within the topic. (Figure 1) Clicking a topic box provides more information. Users can rename topics, label unhelpful or low-quality topics as JUNK, or sort them in terms of frequency in the corpus,[1] predicted quality,[2] or junk.

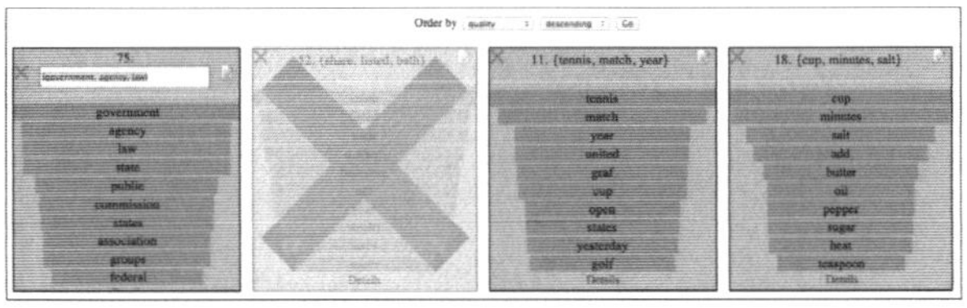

Figure 1: *Topics Page* A view of the first row of topics, and the sorting selector at the top of the page. The left topic is being renamed. The second topic has been marked as junk.

Sarah renames several topics, including the topic "{running, athletes, race}" as SPORTS *and marks the "{share, listed, bath}" topic as* JUNK.

Documents View The document view provides a faceted browsing interface of the corpus. (Figure 2) The pane on the right side displays the set of documents returned by the current filters (search). Each document is summarized by the first 100 words and any quick view metadata. Users can expand documents to see all document metadata, a graph of the distribution of the topics in this document, and a graph of topics distinctive to this document compared to corpus-wide averages.[3]

Sarah begins by looking at the types of documents in the corpus, opening and closing a few documents as she scrolls down the page.

The facets pane on the left side of the page displays the available facets given the current filters. Topics in a drop-down menu can be used to filter given a threshold.

Sarah selects the value "New York City" for the Location attribute and a threshold of 5% for the SPORTS *topic, filtering on both facets.*

Values next to each metadata facet show the number of documents in the current view with those attribute values, which helps tell the user what to ex-

[1]Frequency is computed using topic assignments from a Gibbs sampler (Griffiths and Steyvers, 2004).

[2]Topic quality is given by the entropy of its word distribution. Other options include Mimno and Blei (2011).

[3]The difference of the probability of a topic in the current document and the topic overall, divided by value overall.

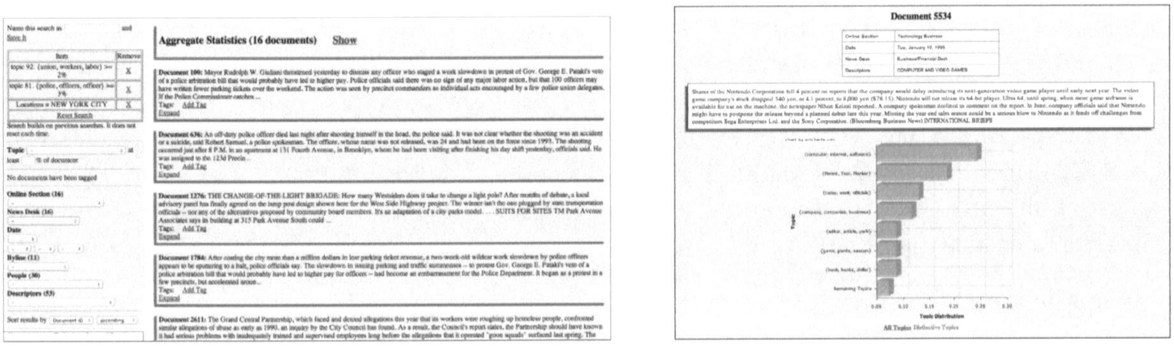

Figure 2: Left: *Documents Page*. The left pane shows the available facets (topics and metadata) and the right pane shows the matching documents (collapsed view.) Right: *Expanded Document*. An expanded collapsed document is replaced with this more detailed view, showing the entire document as well as metadata and topic graphs.

pect if she refines her query.

Sarah notices that the News Desk value of "Sports" matches a large number of documents in the current view. She adds this filter to the current facet query, updating the document view.

At the top of the document pane are the current view's "Aggregate Statistics", which shows how many documents match the current query. An expandable box shows graphs for the current documents topic distribution and distinctive topics.[4]

Looking at the topic graph for the current query, Sarah sees that another topic with sports related words appears with high probability. She adds it to the search and updates the document view.

Any document can be tagged with user-created tags. Tags and their associated documents are displayed in the corpus overview on the configuration page. If a user finds a search query of interest, she can save and name the search to return to it later.

Sarah sees many documents relevant to the New York City Marathon. She tags documents of interest and saves the query for later reference.

2.1 Implementation Details

Our web based tool makes it easy for users to share results, maintain the system, and make the tool widely available. The application is built with a JSP front-end, a Java back-end, and a MongoDB database for storing the corpus and associated data. To ensure a fast UI, filters use an in-memory metadata and topic index. Searches are cached so incremental search queries are very fast. The UI uses Ajax and JQuery UI for dynamic loading and interactive elements. We easily hosted more than a dozen corpora on a single installation.

3 Evaluation

Our primary goal was to investigate whether incorporating topic model output along with document metadata into a faceted browser provided an effective mechanism for filtering documents. Participants were presented with four tasks consisting of a question to answer using the tool and a paragraph providing context. The first three tasks tested exploration (find documents) while the last tested analysis (learn about article authors). At the end of each task, the users were directed to a survey on the tool's usefulness. We also logged user actions to further evaluate how they used the tool.

3.1 Participants and Experimental Setup

Twelve participants (3 female, 9 male) volunteered after receiving an email from a local mailing list. They received no compensation for their participation and they were able to complete the experiment in their preferred environment at a convenient time by accessing the tool online. They were provided with a tool guide and were encouraged to familiarize themselves with the tool before beginning the tasks; logs suggest 8 of 12 did exploration before starting.

The study required participants to find information from a selection of 10,000 documents from the New York Times Annotated Corpus (Sandhaus, 2008), which contains a range of metadata.[5] All

[4] Computed as above but with more topics displayed.

[5] The full list of metadata fields that we allowed users to ac-

documents in the corpus were published in January of 1995 and we made no effort at deduplication. Topics were generated using the Latent Dirichlet Allocation (LDA) (Blei et al., 2003) implementation in MALLET (McCallum, 2002). We used 100 topics trained with 1500 Gibbs iterations and hyper-parameter optimization.

3.2 Quantitative Results

The length of time required to complete individual tasks ranged from 1 minute and 3 seconds to 24 minutes and 54 seconds (average 9 minutes.) [6]

Within the scope of each task, each user initiated on average 5.75 searches. The time between searches was on average 1 minute and 53 seconds. Of all the searches, 21.4% were new searches and 78.6% built on previous searches when users chose to expand or narrow the scope of the search. When users initiated new search queries, they began with queries on topics 59.3% of the time, with queries on metadata 37.3% of the time, and queries that used both topics and metadata 3.4% of the time. This lends credence to the claim that the ability to access both metadata and topics is crucial.

We asked users to rate features in terms of their usefulness on a Likert scale from 1 (not helpful at all) to 5 (extremely helpful). The most preferred features were filtering on topics (mean 4.217, median 5) and compacted documents (mean 3.848, median 5) The least preferred were document graphs of topic usage (mean 1.848, median 1) and aggregate statistics (mean 1.891, median 1).[7] The fact that filtering on topics was the most preferred feature validates our approach of including topics as a facet. Additionally, topic names were critical to this success.

3.3 Surveys

Users provided qualitative feedback[8] by describing their approaches to the task, and offering suggestions, the most common of which was an increase in allowed query complexity, a feature we intend to enhance. In the current version, all search terms are combined using AND; 7 of the 12 participants made requests for a NOT option.

Some users (6 of 12) admitted to using their browser's search feature to help complete the tasks. We chose to forgo a keyword search capability in the study-ready version of the tool because we wanted to test the ability of topic information to provide a way to navigate the content. Given the heavy usage of topic searches and the ability of users to complete tasks with or without browser search, we have demonstrated the usefulness of the topics as a window into the content. In future versions, we envision incorporating keyword search capabilities, including suggested topic filters for searched queries.

As users completed the tasks, their comfort with the tool increased. One user wrote, "After the last task I knew exactly what to do to get my results. I knew what information would help me find documents." Users also began to suggest new ways that they would like to see topics and metadata combined. Task 4 led one user to say "It would be interesting to see a page on each author and what topics they mostly covered." We could provide this in a general way by showing a page for each metadata attribute that contains relevant topics and other metadata. We intend to implement such features.

4 Conclusion

A user evaluation of MetaToMATo, our toolkit for visualizing text corpora that incorporates both topic models and metadata, confirms the validity of our approach to use topic models and metadata in a single faceted browser. Users searched with topics a majority of the time, but also made use of metadata. This clearly demonstrates a reliance on both, suggesting that users went back and forth as needed. Additionally, while metadata is traditionally used for facets, users ranked filtering by topic more highly than metadata. This suggests a new direction in which advances in topic models can be used to aid corpus exploration.

cess in the study was: online section, organization, news desk, date, locations, series name, byline (author), people, title, feature page, and descriptors.

[6]These times do not include the 3 instances in which a user felt unable to complete a task. Also omitted are 11 tasks (from 4 users) for which log files could not provide accurate times.

[7]Ratings are likely influenced by the specific nature of the sample user tasks. In tasks that required seeking out metadata, expanded document views rated higher than their average.

[8]The survey results presented here consist of one survey per participant per task, with two exceptions where two participants each failed to record one of their four surveys.

References

David M. Blei, Andrew Y. Ng, and Michael I. Jordan. 2003. Latent dirichlet allocation. *J. Mach. Learn. Res.*, 3:993–1022, March.

M. Cataldi, L. Di Caro, and C. Schifanella. 2011. Immex: Immersive text documents exploration system. In *Content-Based Multimedia Indexing (CBMI), 2011 9th International Workshop on*, pages 1–6. IEEE.

A.J.B. Chaney and D.M. Blei. 2012. Visualizing topic models. In *AAAI*.

J. Chuang, C.D. Manning, and J. Heer. 2012. Termite: visualization techniques for assessing textual topic models. In *Proceedings of the International Working Conference on Advanced Visual Interfaces*, pages 74–77. ACM.

Christopher Collins, Fernanda B. Viégas, and Martin Wattenberg. 2009. Parallel tag clouds to explore and analyze faceted text corpora. In *Proc. of the IEEE Symp. on Visual Analytics Science and Technology (VAST)*.

M. Correll, M. Witmore, and M. Gleicher. 2011. Exploring collections of tagged text for literary scholarship. *Computer Graphics Forum*, 30(3):731–740.

W. Cui, S. Liu, L. Tan, C. Shi, Y. Song, Z. Gao, H. Qu, and X. Tong. 2011. Textflow: Towards better understanding of evolving topics in text. *Visualization and Computer Graphics, IEEE Transactions on*, 17(12):2412–2421.

W. Dou, X. Wang, R. Chang, and W. Ribarsky. 2011. Paralleltopics: A probabilistic approach to exploring document collections. In *Visual Analytics Science and Technology (VAST), 2011 IEEE Conference on*, pages 231–240. IEEE.

Jacob Eisenstein, Duen Horng "Polo" Chau, Aniket Kittur, and Eric P. Xing. 2012. Topicviz: Interactive topic exploration in document collections. In *CHI*.

Jennifer English, Marti Hearst, Rashmi Sinha, Kirsten Swearingen, and Ka-Ping Yee. 2002. Flexible search and navigation using faceted metadata. In *ACM SIGIR Conference on Information Retrieval (SIGIR)*.

Ko Fujimura, Hiroyuki Toda, Takafumi Inoue, Nobuaki Hiroshima, Ryoji Kataoka, and Masayuki Sugizaki. 2006. Blogranger - a multi-faceted blog search engine. In *World Wide Web (WWW)*.

Matthew J. Gardner, Joshua Lutes, Jeff Lund, Josh Hansen, Dan Walker, Eric Ringger, and Kevin Seppi. 2010. The topic browser: An interactive tool for browsing topic models. In *NIPS Workshop on Challenges of Data Visualization*.

T.L. Griffiths and M. Steyvers. 2004. Finding scientific topics. *Proceedings of the National Academy of Sciences of the United States of America*, 101(Suppl 1):5228–5235.

Marti Hearst. 2006. Clustering versus faceted categories for information exploration. *Communications of the ACM*, 49(4).

Mika Käki. 2005. Findex: search result categories help users when document ranking fails. In *Proceedings of the SIGCHI Conference on Human Factors in Computing Systems*, CHI '05, pages 131–140, New York, NY, USA. ACM.

S. Liu, M.X. Zhou, S. Pan, W. Qian, W. Cai, and X. Lian. 2009. Interactive, topic-based visual text summarization and analysis. In *Proceedings of the 18th ACM conference on Information and knowledge management*, pages 543–552. ACM.

G. Marchionini. 2006. Exploratory search: from finding to understanding. *Communications of the ACM*, 49(4):41–46.

Andrew Kachites McCallum. 2002. Mallet: A machine learning for language toolkit. http://mallet.cs.umass.edu.

D. Mimno and D. Blei. 2011. Bayesian checking for topic models. In *Proceedings of the Conference on Empirical Methods in Natural Language Processing*, pages 227–237. Association for Computational Linguistics.

Eyal Oren, Renaud Delbru, and Stefan Decker. 2006. Extending faceted navigation for rdf data. In *International Semantic Web Conference (ISWC)*.

Evan Sandhaus. 2008. The new york times annotated corpus.

Christian Seeling and Andreas Becks. 2003. Exploiting metadata for ontology-based visual exploration of weakly structured text documents. In *Proceedings of the 7th International Conference on Information Visualisation (IV03*, pages 0–7695. IEEE Press, ISBN.

Greg Smith, Mary Czerwinski, Brian Meyers, Daniel Robbins, George Robertson, and Desney S. Tan. 2006. FacetMap: A Scalable Search and Browse Visualization. *IEEE Transactions on Visualization and Computer Graphics*, 12(5):797–804.

E.M. Talley, D. Newman, D. Mimno, B.W. Herr II, H.M. Wallach, G.A.P.C. Burns, A.G.M. Leenders, and A. McCallum. 2011. Database of nih grants using machine-learned categories and graphical clustering. *Nature Methods*, 8(6):443–444.

Ping Yee, Kirsten Swearingen, Kevin Li, and Marti Hearst. 2003. Faceted metadata for image search and browsing. In *Computer-Human Interaction (CHI)*.

TMTprime: A Recommender System for MT and TM Integration

Aswarth Dara†, Sandipan Dandapat‡,*, Declan Groves† and Josef van Genabith†
† Centre for Next Generation Localisation, School of Computing
Dublin City University, Dublin, Ireland
‡ Department of Computer Science and Engineering
IIT-Guwahati, Assam, India
{adara, dgroves, josef}@computing.dcu.ie, sdandapat@iitg.ernet.in

Abstract

TMTprime is a recommender system that facilitates the effective use of both translation memory (TM) and machine translation (MT) technology within industrial language service providers (LSPs) localization workflows. LSPs have long used Translation Memory (TM) technology to assist the translation process. Recent research shows how MT systems can be combined with TMs in Computer Aided Translation (CAT) systems, selecting either TM or MT output based on sophisticated translation quality estimation without access to a reference. However, to date there are no commercially available frameworks for this. TMTprime takes confidence estimation out of the lab and provides a commercially viable platform that allows for the seamless integration of MT with legacy TM systems to provide the most effective (least effort/cost) translation options to human translators, based on the TMTprime confidence score.

1 Introduction

Within the LSP community there is growing interest in the use of MT as a means to increase automation and reduce overall localisation project cost. When high-quality MT output is available, translators see significant productivity gains over translation from scratch, but poor MT quality leads to frustration and wasted time as suggested translations are discarded in favour of providing a translation from scratch. We present a commercially-relevant software platform providing a translation confidence estimation metric and, based on this, a mechanism for effectively integrating MT with TMs in localisation workflows. The confidence metric ensures that only those MT outputs that are guaranteed to require less post-editing effort than the best corresponding TM match are presented to the post-editor (He et al., 2010a). The MT is integrated seamlessly, and established localisation cost estimation models based on TM technologies still apply as upper bounds.

*Author did this work during his post doctoral research at CNGL.

2 Related Work

MT confidence estimation and its relation to existing TM scoring methods, together with how to make the most effective use of both technologies, is an active area of research.

(Specia, 2011) and (Specia et al., 2009, 2010) propose a confidence estimator that relates specifically to the post-editing effort of translators. This research uses regression on both the automatic scores assigned to the MT and scores assigned by post-editors and aims to model post-editors' judgements of the translation quality between *good* and *bad*, or among three levels of post-editing effort.

Our work is an extension of (He et al., 2010a,b,c), and uses outputs and features relevant to the TM and MT systems. We focus on using system external features. This is important for cases where the internals of the MT system are not available, as in the use of MT as a service in a localisation workflow.[1] Furthermore, instead of having to solve a regression problem, our approach is based on solving an easier binary prediction problem (using Support Vector Machines) and can be easily integrated into TMs. (He et al., 2010b) present a MT/TM segment recommender, (He et al., 2010c) a MT/TM n-best list segment re-ranker and (He et al., 2010a) a MT/TM integration method that can use matching sub-segments in MT/TM combination. Importantly,

[1](Specia et al., 2009) note that using glass-box features when available, in addition to black-box features, offer only small gains and also incur significant computational effort.

translators can tune the models for precision without retraining the models.

Related research by (Simard and Isabelle., 2009) focuses on combining TM information into an SMT system for improving the performance of the MT when a close match already exists within the TM. (Koehn and Haddow, 2009) presents a post-editing environment using information from the phrase-based SMT system Moses.[2] (Guerberof, 2009) compares the post-editing effort required for TM and MT output, respectively. (Tatsumi, 2009) studies the correlation between automatic evaluation scores and post-editing effort.

3 Translation Recommender

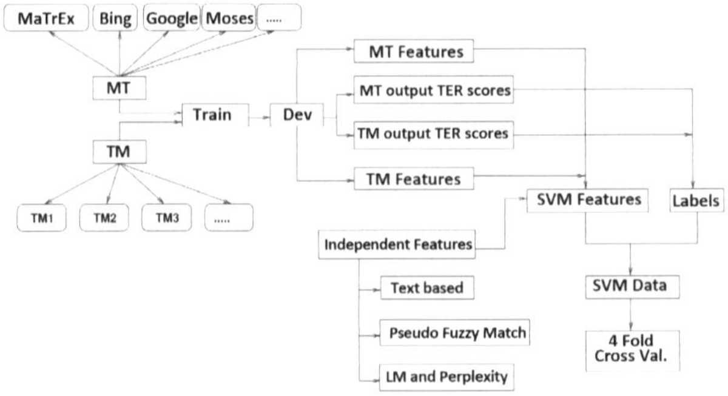

Figure 1: TMTprime Workflow

The workflow of the translation recommender is shown in Figure 1. We train MT systems using a significant portion of the training data and use these models as well as TM outputs to obtain a recommendation development data set. MT systems can be either in-house, e.g. a Moses-based system, or externally available systems, such as Microsoft Bing[3] or Google Translate.[4] For each sentence in the development data set, we have access to the reference as well as to the outputs for each of the MT and TM systems. We then select the best MT (or TM) output as the translation with the lowest TER score with respect to the reference and label the data accordingly. System-independent features for each translation output are fed as input to the SVM classifier (Cortes and Vapnik, 1995). The SVM classifier outputs class labels and the class labels are converted into confidence scores using the techniques given in (Lin et al., 2007). Relying on system independent black-box features has allowed us to build a fully extendable platform that will allow any number of MT systems (or indeed TM systems) to be plugged into the recommender with little effort.

[2]http://www.statmt.org/moses/

[3]http://www.bing.com/translator

[4]http://translate.google.com/

4 Demo Description

Using the Amazon EC2[5] deployment as a back-end, we have developed a front-end GUI for the system (Figure 2). The interface allows the user to select which of the available translation systems (whether they be MT or TM) they wish to use within the recommender system. The user can input their own pre-established estimated cost of post-editing, based on error ranges. Typically the costs for post-editing those translations which have a lower-error rate (i.e. fewer errors) is less than the cost for post-editing translations which have a greater number of errors, as they are of lower quality. The user is requested to upload a file for translation to the system.

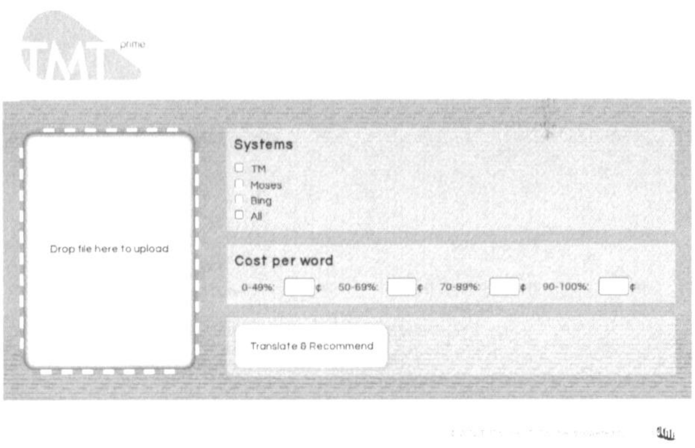

Figure 2: TMTprime GUI

Once the user has selected their desired options, the TMTprime platform provides various analysis measures based on its recommendation engine, such as how many segments from the input file are recommended for translation by the various selected translation engines or TMs available. Based on the input costs, it provides a visualisation of overall estimated cost of either using an individual translation system on its own, or using the recommender selecting the best performing system on a segment-by-segment basis. The TMTprime system is an implementation of a segment-based system selector selecting the most appropriate available translation/TM system for a given input. A snapshot of the results produced by TMTprime is given in Figure 3: the pie-chart shows what percentage of segments are recommended from each of the translation systems; the

[5]http://aws.amazon.com/ec2/

bar-graph gives an estimated cost of using a single translation system alone and the estimated cost when using TMTprime's combined recommendation. The estimated cost using TMTprime is lower when compared to using a single MT or TM system alone (in the worst case, it will be the same as the best-performing single translation engine or TM system). This estimated cost includes both the cost for translation (currently uniform cost for each translation system) and the cost required for post-editing. For example, if the MT is an in-house system the cost of translation will be (close to) zero whereas there is potentially an additional base cost for using an external MT engine. Finally, the interface provides statistics related to various confidence levels for different translation outputs across the various translation and TM systems.

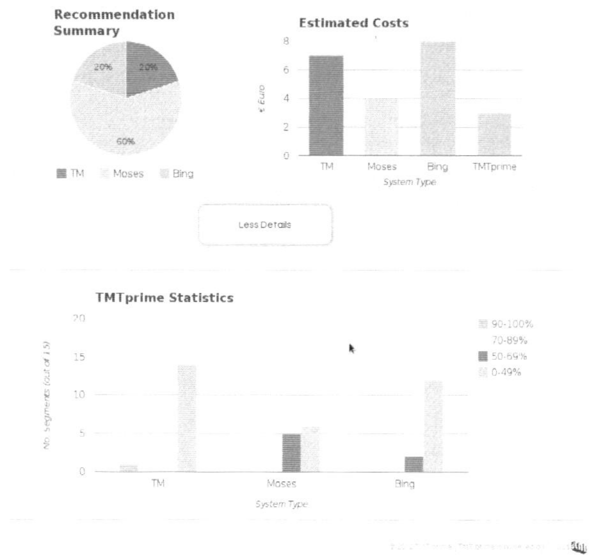

Figure 3: Results shown by TMTprime system

5 Experiments and Results

Evaluation targets two objectives and is described below.

5.1 Correlation with Automatic Metrics

TER and METEOR are widely-used automatic metrics (Snover et al., 2006; Denkowski and Lavie, 2011) that calculate the quality of translation output by comparing it against a human translation, known as the reference translation. Our data sets for the experiment consist of English-French translation memories from the IT domain. In all instances MT was carried out for English-French translations. As we have access to the reference target language translations for our test set, we are able to calculate the TER and METEOR scores for the three translation outputs (here TM, MaTrEx (Dandapat et al., 2010) and Microsoft Bing). For each sentence in the test set, TMTprime recommends a particular translation output with a certain estimated confidence level without access to a reference. We measure Pearson's correlation coefficient (Hollander and Wolfe, 1999) between the recommendation scores, TER scores and METEOR scores (for all system outputs) in order to determine how well the TMTprime prediction score correlates with the widely used automatic evaluation metrics. Results of these experiments are provided in Table 1 which shows there is a negative correlation between TMTprime scores and TER scores. This shows that both TMTprime scores and TER scores are moving in opposite directions, supporting the claim that the higher the recommendation scores, the lower the TER scores. As TER is an error score, the lower the TER score, the higher the quality of the machine translation output compared to its reference. On the other hand, TMTprime scores are positively correlated with METEOR scores which supports the claim that the higher the recommendation scores, the higher the METEOR scores.

Pearson's r	**TER**	**METEOR**
TMTprime	-0.402	0.447

Table 1: Correlation with automatic metrics

The evaluation has been performed on a test data set of 2,500 sentences. Both the correlations are significant at the ($p<0.01$) level.

5.2 Correlation with Post-Editing time

This is the most important and crucial metric for the evaluation. For this experiment we made use of post-editing data captured during a real-world translation task, for English-French in the IT domain.

Pearson's r	**TER**	**METEOR**	**PE Time**
TMTprime	-0.122	0.129	-0.132

Table 2: Correlation with Post-Editing times

For testing, we collect the post-editing times for MT outputs from two different translators using a commercial computer-aided translation (CAT tool) in a real-world production scenario. The data set consists of 1113 samples and is different from the one used in the correlation with automatic metrics.

Post-editing times provide a real measure of the amount of post-editing effort required to perfect the output of the MT system. For this experiment, we took the output of the MT system used in the task together with the post-editing times and measured the Pearsons correlation coefficient between the TMTprime recommendation scores and the post-editing (PE) times (only for MT output from a single system since this data set does contain PE times for other translation outputs). In addition, we also repeated the previous experiment setup for finding the correlation between the TMTprime scores and the automatically-produced TER, METEOR scores for this data set. The results are given in Table 2.

The results show that the confidence scores do correlate with automatic evaluation metrics and post-editing times. Although the correlations do not seem as strong as before, the results are statistically significant ($p<0.01$).

6 Conclusions and Future Work

We present a commercially viable translation recommender system which selects the best output from multiple TM/MT outputs. We have shown that our confidence score correlates with automatic metrics and post-editing times. For future work, we are looking into extending and evaluating the system for different language pairs and data sets.

Acknowledgments

This work is supported by Science Foundation Ireland (Grants SFI11-TIDA-B2040 and 07/CE/I1142) as part of the Centre for Next Generation Localisation (www.cngl.ie) at Dublin City University. We would also like to thank Symantec, Autodesk and Welocalize for their support and provision of data sets used in our experiments.

References

Cortes, Corinna and Vladimir Vapnik. 1995. Support-vector networks. In *Machine Learning*. pages 273–297.

Dandapat, Sandipan, Mikel L. Forcada, Declan Groves, Sergio Penkale, John Tinsley, and Andy Way. 2010. OpenMaTrEx: A free/open-source marker-driven example-based machine translation system. In *Proceedings of the 7th international conference on Advances in natural language processing*. Springer-Verlag, Berlin, Heidelberg, IceTAL'10, pages 121–126.

Denkowski, Michael and Alon Lavie. 2011. Meteor 1.3: Automatic metric for reliable optimization and evaluation of machine translation systems. In *Proceedings of the EMNLP 2011 Workshop on Statistical Machine Translation*. Edinburgh, UK.

Guerberof, Ana. 2009. Productivity and quality in mt post-editing. In *Proceedings of Machine Translation Summit XII - Workshop: Beyond Translation Memories: New Tools for Translators*. Ottawa, Canada.

He, Yifan, Yanjun Ma, J Roturier, Andy Way, and Josef van Genabith. 2010a. Improving the post-editing experience using translation recommendation: A user study. In *Proceedings of the Ninth Conference of the Association for Machine Translation in the Americas*. Denver, Colorado, AMTA 2010, pages 247–256.

He, Yifan, Yanjun Ma, Josef van Genabith, and Andy Way. 2010b. Bridging smt and tm with translation recommendation. In *Proceedings of the 48th Annual Meeting of the Association for Computational Linguistics*. Association for Computational Linguistics, Uppsala, Sweden, ACL 2010, pages 622–630.

He, Yifan, Yanjun Ma, Andy Way, and Josef van Genabith. 2010c. Integrating n-best smt outputs into a tm system. In *Proceedings of the 23rd International Conference on Computational Linguistics: Posters*. Association for Computational Linguistics, Beijing, China, COLING 2010, pages 374–382.

Hollander, Myles and Douglas A. Wolfe. 1999. *Nonparametric Statistical Methods*. John Wiley and Sons.

Koehn, Philip and Barry Haddow. 2009. Interactive assistance to human translators using statistical machine translation methods. In *Proceedings of MT Summit XII*. Ottawa, Canada, pages 73–80.

Lin, Hsuan-Tien, Chih-Jen Lin, and Ruby C. Weng. 2007. A note on platt's probabilistic outputs for support vector machines. *Machine Learning* 68(3):267–276.

Simard, Michael and Pierre Isabelle. 2009. Phrase-based machine translation in a computer-assisted translation environment. In *Proceedings of Machine Translation Summit XII*. Ottawa, Canada, pages 120–127.

Snover, Matthew, Bonnie Dorr, Richard Schwartz, Linnea Micciulla, and John Makhoul. 2006. A study of translation edit rate with targeted human annotation. In *Proceedings of Association for Machine Translation in the Americas*. Cambridge, MA, pages 223–231.

Specia, Lucia. 2011. Exploiting objective annotations for measuring translation post-editing effort. In *Proceedings of the 15th Annual Conference of the European Association for Machine Translation*. Leuven, Belgium, EAMT 2011, pages 73–80.

Specia, Lucia, Nicola Cancedda, and Marc Dymetman. 2010. A dataset for assessing machine translation evaluation metrics. In *Proceedings of LREC 2010*. Valletta, Malta.

Specia, Lucia, Marco Turqui, Zhuoran Wang, John Shawe-Taylor, and Craig Saunders. 2009. Improving the confidence of machine translation quality estimates. In *Proceedings of Machine Translation Summit XII*. Ottawa, Canada, pages 136–143.

Tatsumi, Midori. 2009. Correlation between automatic evaluation scores, post-editing speed and some other factors. In *Proceedings of Machine Translation Summit XII*. Ottawa, Canada, pages 332–339.

Anafora: A Web-based General Purpose Annotation Tool

Wei-Te Chen
Department of Computer Science
University of Colorado at Boulder
weite.chen@colorado.edu

Will Styler
Department of Linguistics
University of Colorado at Boulder
william.styler@colorado.edu

Abstract

Anafora is a newly-developed open source web-based text annotation tool built to be lightweight, flexible, easy to use and capable of annotating with a variety of schemas, simple and complex. Anafora allows secure web-based annotation of any plaintext file with both spanned (e.g. named entity or markable) and relation annotations, as well as adjudication for both types of annotation. Anafora offers automatic set assignment and progress-tracking, centralized and human-editable XML annotation schemas, and file-based storage and organization of data in a human-readable single-file XML format.

1 Introduction

Anafora[1] is a new annotation tool designed to be a lightweight, flexible annotation solution which is easy to deploy for large and small projects. Previous tools (such as Protege/Knowtator (Ogren, 2006) or eHost) have been written primarily with local annotation in mind, running as native, local applications and reading complex file or folder structures. This limits cross-platform deployment and requires the annotated data to be stored locally on machines or run in X-Windows, complicating data-use agreements and increasing data fragmentation.

Anafora was designed as a web-based tool to avoid this issue, allowing multiple anntators to access data remotely from a single instance running on a remote server. Designed for WebKit-based browsers, annotators can work from nearly any modern OS, and no installation, local storage, or SSH logins are required. All data is regularly autosaved, and annotations are saved to cache for restoration in the event of a connectivity interruption.

In addition, avoiding the complex schemas and filetypes associated with many current solutions, Anafora was built to maintain simple, organized representations of the data it generates. Annotation schemas and stored data are both saved as human-readable XML, and these are stored alongside plaintext annotated files in a simple, database-free, static filesystem. This allows easy automated assignment and organization of sets and offers ease of administration and oversight unmatched by other tools.

Most importantly, though, Anafora has been designed to offer an efficient and learnable means for annotation and adjudication using even complex schemas and multi-step workflows (such as UMLS (medical named entity tags), Coreference, and THYME Temporal Relations annotation, described in (Albright et al., 2013)). This allows Anafora to a single-source solution for whole-text annotation across all of your projects.

2 Comparisons with existing tools

Anafora has been designed from the ground up with some key advantages over existing whole-text annotation solutions such as eHost/Chartreader (South et al., 2012), Protege/Knowtator (Ogren, 2006), and BRAT (Stenetorp et al., 2012).

Both Protege and eHost are locally-run Java software (although eHost also relies on a remote in-

[1] Anafora is free and open-source, and is available (along with documentation and sample projects) for public use on *https://github.com/weitechen/anafora*

stall of Chartreader). Although they are available for all major platforms, they require annotators to install the applications locally and upgrade the installations as major issues come up. More importantly, both store the texts being annotated locally on the machine used for annotation, which is problematic under many data-use agreements for medical or otherwise sensitive data. Anafora addresses this shortcoming by its web-based design, allowing easy software update and eliminating local data storage, while also enabling automatic and centralized set assignment.

Another of Anafora's strengths over existing tools is flexibility and complex schema support. At last review, eHost/Chartreader offered only rudimentary between-annotation relations (primarily for coreference), lacking the flexibility needed for more complex relation sets. BRAT does offer an effective relation annotation tool, but doesn't support the more complex schemas and property types that Anafora does (e.g. multi-slot relations, relation properties, pointers as properties of entities, etc). So, although both BRAT and eHost/Chartreader are excellent solutions for simple annotation schemas, for complex schemas and workflows, Anafora is a more flexible and capable choice.

Finally, Anafora's biggest strength is its lightweight implementation. Unlike Protege/Knowator's folder model where each assigned annotation task contains a separate copy of the schema, document, and project, Anafora's folders-containing-XML model of document and schema storage means that each document and schema is stored only once in one easily accessible place, and unlike eHost/Chartreader, administration can be done by changing and moving files from SFTP or a command line, rather than by logging in to a separate program. This central storage means that schema modification is as easy as changing one XML file, which will be used for all subsequent annotations, and the file-based model eliminates the need to back up large databases.

In short, although many annotation tools exist, Anafora's combination of light weight, web-based UI, centralized file storage and complex schema support make Anafora unique and an excellent choice for any annotation project.

```
<definition>
 <entities type="TemporalEntities" color="015367">
  <entity type="EVENT" color="00ccff" hotkey="e">
   <properties>
    <property type="DocTimeRel" input="choice">
     ,BEFORE,OVERLAP,AFTER,BEFORE/OVERLAP</property>
    <property type="Type" input="choice">
     N/A,ASPECTUAL</property>
    ......</properties></entity>
  .......</entities>
 <relations type="TemporalRelations" color="0000ff">
  <relation type="TLINK" color="0000ff" hotkey="l">
   <properties>
    <property type="Source" input="list"
      maxlink="1" instanceOf="EVENT,TIMEX3"/>
    <property type="Target" input="list"
      maxlink="1" instanceOf="EVENT,TIMEX3"/>
   ......</properties></relation>
 ......</relations></definition>
```

Figure 1: Anafora Schema Example

3 Schema and Data Format

In Anafora, annotations are divided into two types: *Entity* and *Relation*. An *Entity* annotation associates a certain span in the text with a type and list of properties. *Relation* annotations specify a relationship between multiple *Entities*. The nature of these *Entity* and *Relation* annotations (as well as their properties) are stored in an XML Schema file, while data files store the *Entities* and *Relations* specified by annotators for each file.

3.1 Schema

The schema file defines the data type and attributes of the annotations. Our schema format is defined in XML form, which is a simple and human-readable markup file. A Temporal schema is shown in Fig. 1.

The first part of the schema file is "defaultattribute" element in which the schema's overall attributes are defined. Another part is the "definition" element which defines the hierarchy of the schema tree, the annotation types, and the associated properties for each type. The schema is in the form of a tree structure. The "entities" and "relations" tags represent subgroupings of annotation types, while the "entity" and "relation" tags each define a different *Entity* or *Relation* annotation. The "type" attribute defines the name of the annotation type, the "color" attribute defines the displayed color of this annotation in the Anafora interface, and the "hotkey" attribute is the key which triggers creation of that an-

```
<entity>
 <id>5@e@ID020_clinic_058@gold</id>
 <span>1328,1342</span>
 <type>EVENT</type>
 <parentsType>TemporalEntities</parentsType>
 <properties>
  <DocTimeRel>BEFORE</DocTimeRel>
  <Type>N/A</Type>
  ......</properties></entity>
......
<relation>
 <id>2@r@ID020_clinic_058@gold</id>
 <type>TLINK</type>
 <parentsType>TemporalRelations</parentsType>
  <properties>
  <Source>5@e@ID020_clinic_058@gold</Source>
  <Target>7@e@ID020_clinic_058@gold</Target>
  <Type>CONTAINS</Type>
 </properties></relation>
```

Figure 2: Anafora Data File Example

notation in Anafora.

For each type, the properties to be annotated are listed under "Property", where the "type" attribute indicates the name of the property, while the "input" attribute specifies the manner of attribute selection or entry. The value of the "Property" is a list of accepted choices. For example, the "Type" property in the "Event" entity limits the value to "N/A" or "ASPECTUAL", where "N/A" is the default. Please refer to the Guidelines for further detail.

One great advantage of this XML-based schema format is greater flexibility than existing tools both in schema and modification. To make any modification to the schema, one simply edits the XML and the revised schema will apply to any new data files. Another advantage is human-readability, allowing schemas to be easily understood and ported from other tools.

3.2 Data File

The Anafora data file (see Fig. 2) stores the annotation instances for each annotated file. It, like the Schema file, uses an XML format.

The "info" section provides the basic information for the file, such as the save time and annotation completion status. The "schema" tag specifies the path to the schema file used for annotation. Following is the "annotation." Each "entity" and "relation" element represents an annotation instance. Every annotation has a unique "id", and the annotation "type" and "parentType". For *Entity* annotations, the text's span is given using character offsets in the source file. For all annotations, the "property" section specifies the values for properties listed in the schema, and, for *Relations*, properties are used ("Source" and "Target" above) to point to the unique IDs of the annotations being linked.

4 System Overview

Anafora is a web-based tool, developed using Django (a Python framework on server side) and jQuery (a JavaScript library on client side). On the server side, our system manages file storage and user access control. By avoiding the use of any database, Anafora is very agile and flexible, and most of the computing work is executed by the user's browser. And, because modern browsers have done an excellent job tuning JavaScript execution, Anafora is lightweight on the user's machine as well. Anafora's browser-based design also allows the tool to run well on any OS with a web browser, alleviating the cross-platform issues common with other tools.

Anafora allows both keyboard- and mouse-based annotation, improving both efficiency and immediate familiarity, rather than relying primarily on mouse-clicks.

Anafora also assists project supervisors in several ways. First, all data management is file-based, and the project hierarchy is reflected in the OS level file system's directory structure. Secondly, Anafora assigns tasks to annotators automatically, saving supervisors the time and hassle of task assignment. Finally, Anafora makes pre-annotation extremely easy. By running the document text through a shallow parser and generating a file which marks all noun phrases (for example), annotators could start their work on a named entity task with this information ready at hand.

Anafora allows users to customize their own user interface by overriding the CSS file on the client side. By changing the CSS file, users can modify the apperance, e.g., color, font, and page layout.

5 Project Creation and Administration

Administering and creating new projects is straightforward, and primarily file based. To create a new project, one first uses our schema markup to write an XML schema designating the entities, relations, and annotation properties needed in the schema (see Section 3). Then, a folder is created for the project, containing folders for any subcorpora, and then finally each document is placed into its own folder as a plaintext file. At this point, annotators with the necessary permissions may select the new schema and documents and begin annotating.

A given document's assignments and completion status is read entirely from the filenames generated by the program. To re-assign a set manually, simply change the annotator's name in the existing annotation file's name, or delete the previous annotation file, allowing Anafora to reassign it automatically. Administrators can view any annotator's work through the tool's interface, and can edit the XML at any time. When a document is fully annotated or adjudicated, preparing for release is as easy as copying the .gold. file and source text into the final destination.

6 Annotation using Anafora

When an annotator opens Anafora in any webkit-based browser and logs in, they are greeted with a file-choosing interface which allows them to pick which corpus, annotation schema and annotation type (*Entity* or *Relation*) they'd like to work on for the session (allowing one annotator to easily work with more than one project or schema). Previously completed and in-progress sets are shown in separate columns for easy access, and only documents which have fewer than the maximum number of annotators are displayed. Annotators are not able to open or view any annotations other than their own.

Once a document is opened, the annotator is presented with Anafora's 3-pane view (in Fig. 3): on the left, the annotation schema, in the center, the source text, and on the right, annotation details. To proceed with an *Entity* annotation, the annotator selects a word or portion of text and hits a pre-defined hotkey, triggering the creation of a new annotation of a specified type, using the selected span.

The properties of the annotation are then automatically filled in with the default values specified in the schema files, and the annotator can then go back in to modify these properties (by drop-down menu, radio buttons, relation or free-text entry) as needed. The annotator can also use the span editing tools to either modify the span character-by-character, or to add a second, disjoint span by selecting more text and using the "+" button.

For *Relation* annotation, the annotator will enable the Relation grid, displaying a list of relations in order of occurrence in the text. To create a new relation, the annotator strikes the proper hotkey, and then Anafora hides all entities which are not allowed to fill slots in this relation. Clicking an entity after pressing "1" fills the first slot, and pressing "2" before a click fills the second slot. As with *Entity* annotations, properties are filled in according to default values in the schema and can be edited as needed.

Annotators can choose to manually save and log out at any point, and when an annotator has completed a document, he or she selects "Mark as Completed", which changes the file's status and queues it up for adjudication.

6.1 Adjudication

When a designated adjudicator logs into Anafora, they're presented with the "Adjudication" annotation type option in the initial document selection screen. When this is selected, only documents with two completed annotator-copies are displayed as available for adjudication.

Once an available document is opened, Anafora will automatically merge the two annotators' work into a new, adjudication datafile (preserving the separate annotations), and then mark as gold any annotations matching for both span and properties. In addition, Anafora will mark as conflicting any annotation pairs with either 1) matching properties and overlapping spans or 2) identical spans and different properties. Anafora then displays the schema and source documents as before along with two annotation detail panes, one for each annotator in a conflicting annotation. A progress bar displays the number of gold annotations out of the total number in the document, and again, progress is automatically saved.

The adjudicator can then use the keyboard to move through the unadjudicated (non-Gold) annotations. When an annotation with a conflict is found, details about both annotations will show up on the right, highlighting in red any areas which differ (span, a property, etc). The adjudicator can then use the arrow keys to select either the left

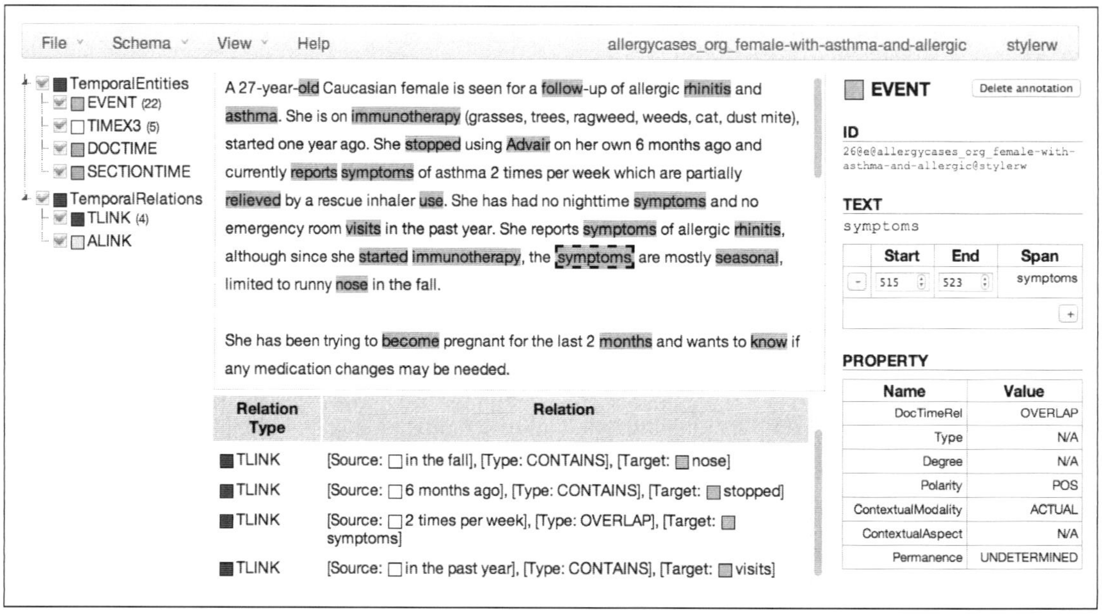

Figure 3: Anafora Annotation Window

or right annotation as Gold, which will delete the other. For single-annotator annotations, the adjudicator can choose to simply delete or mark as Gold.

Once no unadjudicated annotations remain in the document and any necessary edits or additions are made, the adjudicator can mark the document as completed, which changes all annotations' status to "Gold" and, where required, makes the document available to the next round of annotation.

7 Conclusion and Future Work

Anafora can be extended readily to offer other classification tasks such as part-of-speech tags or sense tags. However, there are a couple of limitations. First, tree-based annotation, much like constituent-based semantic role labeling, is not currently supported in Anafora. Additional text information (e.g. Frame files and WordNet ontologies) is difficult to display in the same page as the annotations, as the tool was designed for whole-text annotation. Some complicated schema definitions, such as relations (or relation properties) linking to relations, are also not provided.

We are continuing active development (focusing on annotation efficiency and UX design) as more projects with varied needs use Anafora. Performance studies and comparisons are currently in progress. Furthermore, an administrator interface, including annotator management, task status management, and schema editor, will be supplied. In addition, automated pre-annotation is being incorporated into Anafora-based workflows. We will also allow comparison of annotators' work to extracted annotation characteristics from gold data and from each annotator's prior work. We would also like to include active learning and allow annotators to compare their completed annotations to gold standard data. These features should help to improve the learning and annotation efficiency of the annotators.

Anafora is a lightweight and efficient tool for text annotation, easily adaptable to fit even the most complex of annotation tasks and schemas. Source code is available at our GitHub page, *https://github.com/weitechen/anafora*.

Acknowledgments

The development of this annotation tool was supported by award numbers NLM R0110090 (THYME) and 90TR002 (SHARP), as well as DARPA FA8750-09-C-0179 (via BBN) Machine Reading. The content is solely the responsibility of the authors and does not necessarily represent the official views of the NLM/NIH or DARPA. We would also like to especially thank Jinho Choi for his input on the data format, schemas, and UI/UX.

References

Daniel Albright, Arrick Lanfranchi, Anwen Fredriksen, William Styler, Collin Warner, Jena Hwang, Jinho Choi, Dmitriy Dligach, Rodney Nielsen, James Martin, Wayne Ward, Martha Palmer, and Guergana Savova. 2013. Towards comprehensive syntactic and semantic annotations of the clinical narrative. *Journal of the American Medical Informatics Association. 2013;0:1-9. doi: 10.1136/amiajnl-2012-001317.*

Philip V. Ogren. 2006. Knowtator: A protégé plugin for annotated corpus construction. In *Proceedings of the NAACL-HLT, Companion Volume: Demonstrations*, pages 273–275, New York City, USA, June. Association for Computational Linguistics.

Brett R. South, Shuying Shen, Jianwei Leng, Tyler B. Forbush, Scott L. DuVall, and Wendy W. Chapman. 2012. A prototype tool set to support machine-assisted annotation. In *Proceedings of the 2012 Workshop on Biomedical Natural Language Processing*, BioNLP '12, pages 130–139, Stroudsburg, PA, USA. Association for Computational Linguistics.

Pontus Stenetorp, Sampo Pyysalo, Goran Topić, Tomoko Ohta, Sophia Ananiadou, and Jun'ichi Tsujii. 2012. Brat: a web-based tool for nlp-assisted text annotation. In *Proceedings of the Demonstrations at EACL-2012*, pages 102–107, Avignon, France, April. Association for Computational Linguistics.

A Web Application for the Diagnostic Evaluation of Machine Translation over Specific Linguistic Phenomena

Antonio Toral Sudip Kumar Naskar Joris Vreeke Federico Gaspari Declan Groves
School of Computing
Dublin City University
Ireland
{atoral, snaskar, fgaspari, dgroves}@computing.dcu.ie joris.vreeke@dcu.ie

Abstract

This paper presents a web application and a web service for the diagnostic evaluation of Machine Translation (MT). These web-based tools are built on top of DELiC4MT, an open-source software package that assesses the performance of MT systems over user-defined linguistic phenomena (lexical, morphological, syntactic and semantic). The advantage of the web-based scenario is clear; compared to the standalone tool, the user does not need to carry out any installation, configuration or maintenance of the tool.

1 Automatic Evaluation of Machine Translation beyond Overall Scores

Machine translation (MT) output can be evaluated using different approaches, which can essentially be divided into human and automatic, both of which, however, present a number of shortcomings. Human evaluation tends to be more reliable in a number of ways and can be tailored to a variety of situations, but is rather expensive (both in terms of resources and time) and is difficult to replicate. On the other hand, standard automatic MT evaluation metrics such as BLEU (Papineni et al., 2002) and METEOR (Banerjee and Lavie, 2005) are considerably cheaper and provide faster results, but return rather crude scores that are difficult to interpret for MT users and developers alike. Crucially, current standard automatic MT evaluation metrics also lack any diagnostic value, i.e. they cannot identify specific weaknesses in the MT output. Diagnostic information can be extremely valuable for MT developers and users, e.g. to improve the performance of the system or to decide which output is more suited for particular scenarios.

An interesting alternative to the traditional MT evaluation metrics is to evaluate the performance of MT systems over specific linguistic phenomena. While retaining the main advantage of automatic metrics (low cost), this approach provides more fine-grained linguistically-motivated evaluation. The linguistic phenomena, also referred to as linguistic checkpoints, can be defined in terms of linguistic information at different levels (lexical, morphological, syntactic, semantic, etc.) that appear in the source language. Examples of such linguistic checkpoints, what translation information they can represent, and their relevance for MT are provided in Table 1.

Checkpoint	Relevance for MT
Lexical	Words that can have multiple translations in the target. For example, the preposition "de" in Spanish can be translated into English as "of" or "from" depending on the context.
Syntactic	Syntactic constructs that are difficult to translate. E.g., a checkpoint containing the sequence a noun (*noun1*) followed by the preposition "de", followed by another noun (*noun2*) when translating from Spanish to English. The equivalent English construct would be *noun2*'s *noun1*, the translation thus involving some reordering.
Semantic	Words with multiple meanings, which possibly correspond to different translations in the target language. Polysemous words can be collected from electronic dictionaries such as WordNet (Miller, 1995).

Table 1: Linguistic Checkpoints

Checkpoints can also be built by combining elements from different categories. For example, by combining lexical and syntantic elements, we could define a checkpoint for prepositional phrases (syntactic element) which start with the preposition "de" (lexical element).

Woodpecker (Zhou et al., 2008) is a tool that performs diagnostic evaluation of MT systems over linguistic checkpoints for English–Chinese. Probably due to its limitation to one language pair, its proprietary nature as well as rather restrictive licensing conditions, Woodpecker does not seem to have been widely used in the community, in spite of its ability to support diagnostic evaluation.

DELiC4MT[1] is an open-source software that follows the same approach as Woodpecker. However, DELiC4MT is easily portable to any language pair[2] and provides additional functionality such as filtering of noisy checkpoint instances and support for statistical significance tests. This paper focuses on the usage of this tool through a web application and a web service from the user's perspective. Details regarding its implementation, evaluation, etc. can be found in (Toral et al., 2012; Naskar et al., 2011).

2 Web Services for Language Technology Tools

There exist many freely available language processing tools, some of which are distributed under open-source licenses. In order to use these tools, they need to be downloaded, installed, configured and maintained, which results in high cost both in terms of manual effort and computing resources. The requirement for in-depth technical knowledge severely limits the usability of these tools amongst non-technical users, particularly in our case amongst translators and post-editors.

Web services introduce a new paradigm in the way we use software tools where only providers of the tools are required to have knowledge regarding their installation, configuration and maintenance. This enables wider adoption of the tools and reduces the learning curve for users as the only information needed is basic knowledge of the functionality and input/output parameters (which can be easily included, e.g. as part of an online tutorial). While this paradigm is rather new in the field of computational linguistics, it is quite mature and successful in other fields such as bioinformatics (Oinn et al., 2004; Labarga et al., 2007).

Related work includes two web applications in the area of MT evaluation. iBLEU (Madnani, 2011) organises BLEU scoring information in a visual manner. Berka et al. (2012) perform automatic error detection and classification of MT output.

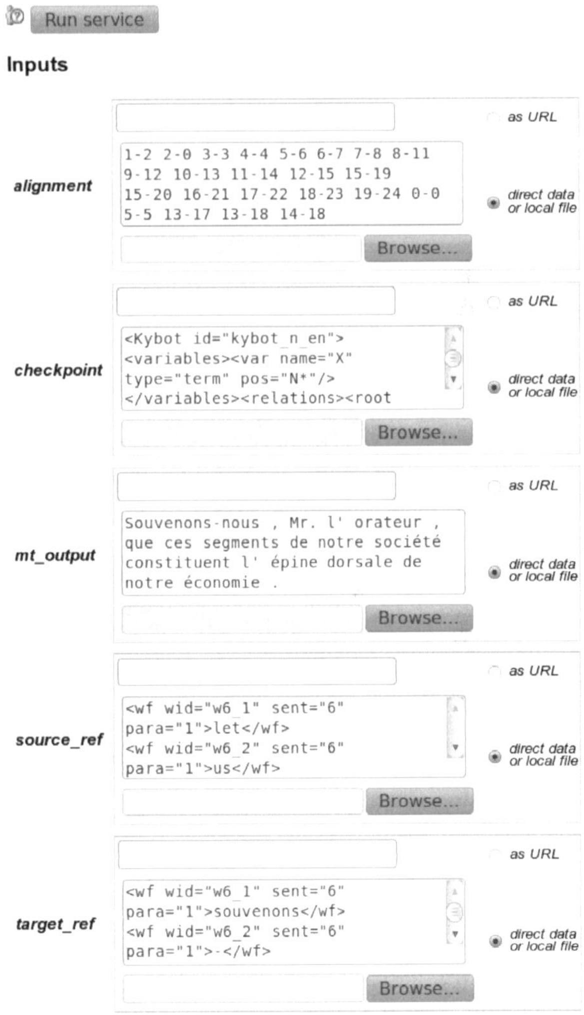

Figure 1: Web interface for the web service.

3 Demo

The demo presented in this paper consists of a web service and a web application built on top of DELiC4MT that allow to assess the performance of MT systems on different linguistic phenomena de-

[1] http://www.computing.dcu.ie/~atoral/delic4mt/

[2] It has already been tested on language pairs involving the following languages: Arabic, Bulgarian, Dutch, English, French, German, Hindi, Italian, Turkish and Welsh.

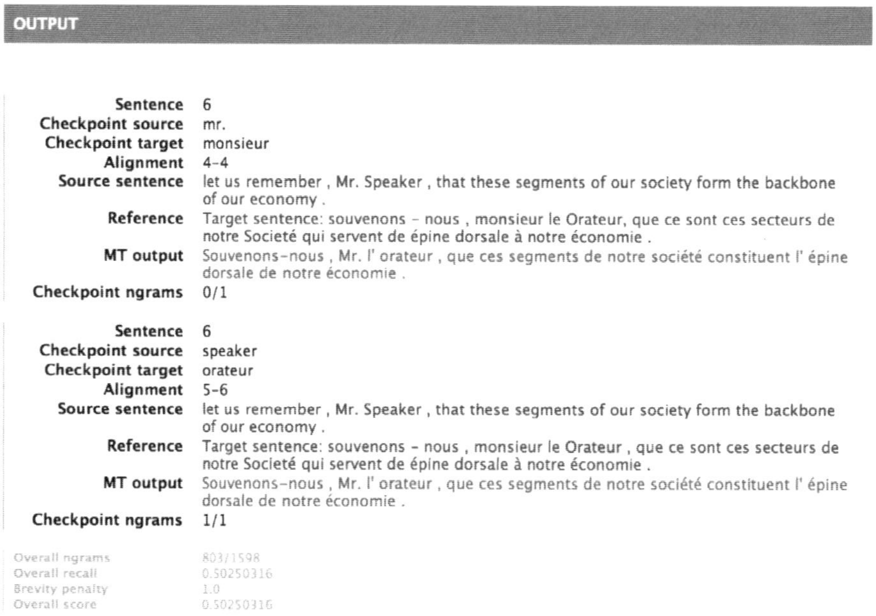

Figure 2: Screenshot of the web application (visualisation of results).

fined by the user. The following subsections detail both parts of the demo.

3.1 Web Service

A SOAP-compliant web service[3] has been built on top of DELiC4MT. It receives the following input parameters (see Figure 1):

1. Word alignment between the source and target sides of the testset, in the GIZA++ (Och and Ney, 2003) output format.
2. Linguistic checkpoint defined as a Kybot[4] (Vossen et al., 2010) profile.
3. Output of the MT system to be evaluated, in plain text, tokenised and one sentence per line.
4. Source and target sides of the testset (or gold standard), in KAF format (Bosma et al., 2009).[5]

The tool then evaluates the performance of the MT system (input parameter 3) on the linguistic phenomenon (parameter 2) by following this procedure:

- Occurrences of the linguistic phenomenon (parameter 2) are identified in the source side of the testset (parameter 4).
- The equivalent tokens of these occurrences in the target side (parameter 5) are found by using word alignment information (parameter 1).
- For each checkpoint instance, the tool checks how many of the n-grams present in the reference of the checkpoint instance are contained in the output produced by the MT system (parameter 3).

3.2 Web Application

The web application builds a graphical interface on top of the web service. It allows the user to visualise the results in a fine-grained manner, the user can see the performance of the MT system for each single occurrence of the linguistic phenomenon.

Sample MT output for the "noun" checkpoint for the English to French language direction is shown in Figure 2. Two occurrences of the checkpoint are shown. The first one regards the source noun "mr." and its translation in the reference "monsieur", identified through word alignments. The alignment (4-4) indicates that both the source and target tokens appear at the fifth position (0-based index) in the sentence. The reference token ("monsieur") is not found in the MT output and thus a score of $0/1$

[3] `http://registry.elda.org/services/301`

[4] Kybot profiles can be understood as regular expressions over KAF documents, `http://kyoto.let.vu.nl/svn/kyoto/trunk/modules/mining_module/`

[5] An XML format for text analysis based on representation standards from ISO TC37/SC4.

(0 n-gram matches out of a total of 1 possible n-gram) is assigned to the MT system for this noun instance. Conversely, the score for the second occurrence ("speaker") is $1/1$ since the MT output contains the 1-gram of the reference translation ("orateur").

The recall-based overall score is shown at the bottom of the figure (0.5025). This is calculated by summing up the scores (matching n-grams) for all the occurrences (803) and dividing the result by the total number of possible n-grams (1598).

4 Conclusions

In this paper we have presented a web application and a web service for the diagnostic evaluation of MT output over linguistic phenomena using DELiC4MT. The tool allows users and developers of MT systems to easily receive fine-grained feedback on the performance of their MT systems over linguistic checkpoints of their interest. The application is open-source, freely available and adaptable to any language pair.

Acknowledgments

The research leading to these results has received funding from the European Union Seventh Framework Programme FP7/2007-2013 under grant agreements FP7-ICT-4-248531 and PIAP-GA-2012-324414 and through Science Foundation Ireland as part of the CNGL (grant 07/CE/I1142)

References

Satanjeev Banerjee and Alon Lavie. 2005. METEOR: An Automatic Metric for MT Evaluation with Improved Correlation with Human Judgments. In *Intrinsic and Extrinsic Evaluation Measures for Machine Translation and/or Summarization, Proceedings of the ACL-05 Workshop*, pages 65–72, University of Michigan, Ann Arbor, Michigan, USA.

Jan Berka, Ondej Bojar, Mark Fishel, Maja Popovi, and Daniel Zeman. 2012. Automatic MT Error Analysis: Hjerson Helping Addicter. In *Proceedings of the Eight International Conference on Language Resources and Evaluation (LREC'12)*, Istanbul, Turkey. European Language Resources Association (ELRA).

W. E. Bosma, Piek Vossen, Aitor Soroa, German Rigau, Maurizio Tesconi, Andrea Marchetti, Monica Monachini, and Carlo Aliprandi. 2009. KAF: a generic semantic annotation format. In *Proceedings of the GL2009 Workshop on Semantic Annotation*, September.

Alberto Labarga, Franck Valentin, Mikael Andersson, and Rodrigo Lopez. 2007. Web services at the european bioinformatics institute. *Nucleic Acids Research*, 35(Web-Server-Issue):6–11.

Nitin Madnani. 2011. iBLEU: Interactively Debugging and Scoring Statistical Machine Translation Systems. In *Proceedings of the 2011 IEEE Fifth International Conference on Semantic Computing*, ICSC '11, pages 213–214, Washington, DC, USA. IEEE Computer Society.

George A. Miller. 1995. WordNet: a lexical database for English. *Commun. ACM*, 38(11):39–41, November.

Sudip Kumar Naskar, Antonio Toral, Federico Gaspari, and Andy Way. 2011. A Framework for Diagnostic Evaluation of MT based on Linguistic Checkpoints. In *Proceedings of the 13th Machine Translation Summit*, pages 529–536, Xiamen, China, September.

Franz Josef Och and Hermann Ney. 2003. A systematic comparison of various statistical alignment models. *Computational Linguistics*, 29:19–51, March.

Tom Oinn, Matthew Addis, Justin Ferris, Darren Marvin, Martin Senger, Mark Greenwood, Tim Carver, Kevin Glover, Matthew R. Pocock, Anil Wipat, and Peter Li. 2004. Taverna: a tool for the composition and enactment of bioinformatics workflows. *Bioinformatics*, 20(17):3045–3054, November.

Kishore Papineni, Salim Roukos, Todd Ward, and Wei-Jing Zhu. 2002. Bleu: a method for automatic evaluation of machine translation. In *Proceedings of the 40th Annual Meeting on Association for Computational Linguistics*, ACL '02, pages 311–318, Stroudsburg, PA, USA. Association for Computational Linguistics.

Antonio Toral, Sudip Kumar Naskar, Federico Gaspari, and Declan Groves. 2012. DELiC4MT: A Tool for Diagnostic MT Evaluation over User-defined Linguistic Phenomena. *The Prague Bulletin of Mathematical Linguistics*, pages 121–132.

Piek Vossen, German Rigau, Eneko Agirre, Aitor Soroa, Monica Monachini, and Roberto Bartolini. 2010. KYOTO: an open platform for mining facts. In *Proceedings of the 6th Workshop on Ontologies and Lexical Resources*, pages 1–10, Beijing, China.

Ming Zhou, Bo Wang, Shujie Liu, Mu Li, Dongdong Zhang, and Tiejun Zhao. 2008. Diagnostic evaluation of machine translation systems using automatically constructed linguistic check-points. In *Proceedings of the 22nd International Conference on Computational Linguistics - Volume 1*, COLING '08, pages 1121–1128, Stroudsburg, PA, USA. Association for Computational Linguistics.

KooSHO: Japanese Text Input Environment based on Aerial Hand Writing

Masato Hagiwara
Rakuten Institute of Technology
215 Park Avenue South,
New York, NY, USA 10003
masato.hagiwara@mail.rakuten.com

Soh Masuko
Rakuten Institute of Technology
4-13-9 Higashi-shinagawa
Shinagawa-ku, Tokyo, JAPAN 140-0002
so.masuko@mail.rakuten.com

Abstract

Hand gesture-based input systems have been in active research, yet most of them focus only on single character recognition. We propose KooSHO: an environment for Japanese input based on aerial hand gestures. The system provides an integrated experience of character input, Kana-Kanji conversion, and search result visualization. To achieve faster input, users only have to input consonant, which is then converted directly to Kanji sequences by *direct consonant decoding*. The system also shows suggestions to complete the user input. The comparison with voice recognition and a screen keyboard showed that KooSHO can be a more practical solution compared to the existing system.

1 Introduction

In mobile computing, intuitive and natural text input is crucial for successful user experience, and there have been many methods and systems proposed as the alternatives to traditional keyboard-and-mouse input devices. One of the most widely used input technologies is voice recognition such as Apple Inc.'s *Siri*. However, it has some drawbacks such as being vulnerable to ambient noise and privacy issues when being overheared. Virtual keyboards[1] require extensive practice and could be error-prone compared to physical keyboards.

Figure 1: Overall text input procedure using KooSHO — (a) Character recognition (b) Kana-Kanji conversion results (c) Search results

In order to address these issues, many gesture-based text input interfaces have been proposed, including a magnet-based hand writing device (Han et al., 2007). Because these systems require users to wear or hold special devices, hand gesture recognition systems based on video cameras are proposed, such as Yoon et al. (1999) and Sonoda and Muraoka (2003). However, a large portion of the literature only focuses on single character input. One must consider overall text input experience when users are typing words and phrases. This problem is pronounced for languages which require explicit conversion from Romanized forms to ideographic writing systems such as Japanese.

In this paper, we propose *KooSHO*: an integrated environment for Japanese text input based on aerial hand gestures. It provides an integrated experience of character input, Kana-Kanji conversion, i.e., conversion from Romanized forms to ideographic (Kanji) ones, and search result visualization. Figure 1 shows the overall procedure using KooSHO. First, (a) a user draws alphabetical shapes in the air, whose hand position is captured by Microsoft Kinect. KooSHO then recognizes characters, and after

[1] http://www.youtube.com/watch?v=h9htRy0-sUw

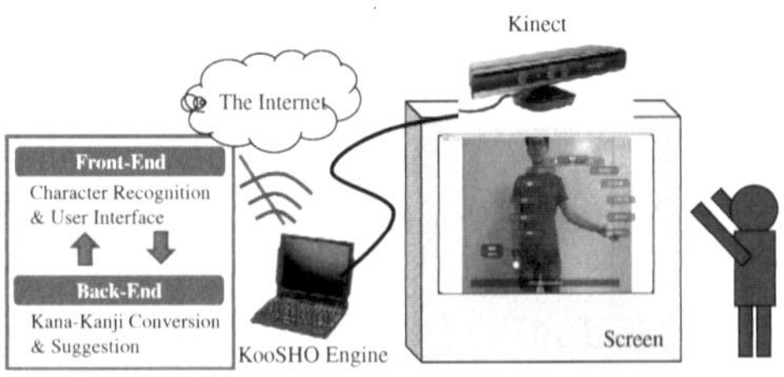

Figure 2: Confiugration of the KooSHO system

Kana-Kanji conversion, the results are shown in a circle centered at the user's shoulder (b). Finally, the user can choose one of the candidates by "touching" it, and (c) the search result using the chosen word as the query is shown in circle again for the user to choose.

KooSHO has several novelties to achieve seamless yet robust text input, including:

Non-restrictive character forms — the system does not restrict on the input character forms, unlike Graffiti 2[2].

Robust continuous recognition and conversion — Aerial handwriting poses special difficulties since the system cannot obtain individual strokes. We solve this problem by employing a discriminative Kana-Kanji conversion model trained on the specific domain.

Faster input by suggestions and consonant input — KooSHO shows suggestions to predict the words the user is about to input, while it allows users to type only consonants, similar to Tanaka-Ishii et al. (2001). We propose *direct consonant decoding*, which runs Viterbi search directly on the input consonant sequence without converting them back into Kana candidates.

We conducted the evaluations on character recognition and Kana-Kanji conversion accuracy to measure KooSHO's performance. We also ran an overall user experience test, comparing its performance with the voice recognition software *Siri* and a screen keyboard.

2 Character Recognition

Figure 2 describes the overall configuration. A user draws alphabetical shapes in the air, which is captured by Kinect and sent to KooSHO. We used the skeleton recognition functionalities included in Kinect for Windows SDK v1.5.1. The system consists of the front-end and back-end parts, which are responsible for character recognition and user interface, and Kana-Kanji conversion and suggestion, respectively.

[2]http://en.wikipedia.org/wiki/Graffiti_2

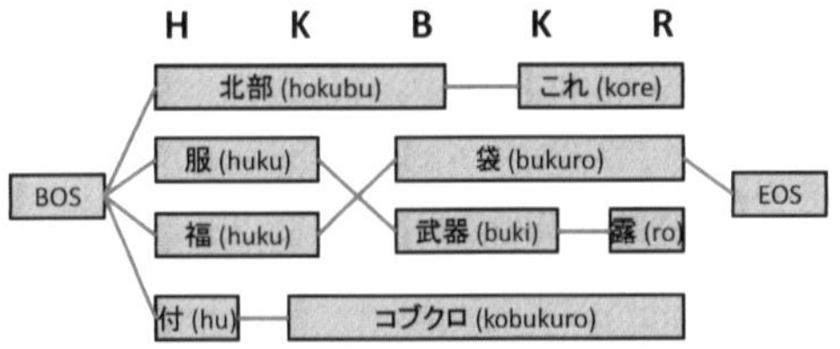

Figure 3: Lattice search based on consonants

We continuously match the drawn trajectory to templates (training examples) using dynamic programming. The trajectory and the templates are both represented by 8 direction features to facilitate the match, and the distance is calculated based on how apart the directions are. This coding system is robust to scaling of characters and a slight variation of writing speed, while not robust to stroke order. This is repeated every frame to produce the distance between the trajectory ending at the current frame and each template. If the distance is below a certain threshold, the character is considered to be the one the user has just drawn.

If more than one characters are detected and their periods overlap, they are both sent as alternative. The result is represented as a lattice, with alternation and concatenation. To each letter a confidence score (the inverse of the minimum distance from the template) is assigned.

3 Kana-Kanji Conversion

In this section, we describe the Kana-Kanji conversion model we employed to achieve the consonant-to-Kanji conversion. As we mentioned, the input to the back-end part passed from the front-end part is a lattice of possible consonant sequences. We therefore have to "guess" the possibly omitted vowels somehow and convert the sequences back into intended Kanji sequences. However, it would be an exponentially large number if we expand the input consonant sequence to all possible Kana sequences. Therefore, instead of attempting to restore all possible Kana sequences, we directly "decode" the input consonant sequence to obtain the Kanji sequence. We call this process *direct consonant decoding*, shown in Figure 3. It is basically the same as the vanilla Viterbi search often used for Japanese morphological analysis (Kudo et al., 2004), except that it runs on a consonant sequence. The key change to this Viterbi search is to make it possible to look up the dictionary directly by consonant substrings. To do this, we convert dictionary entries to possible consonant sequences referring to Microsoft IME Kana Table[3] when the dictionary structure is loaded onto the memory. For example, for a dictionary entry 福袋/フクブクロ *hukubukuro*, possible consonant sequences such as "hkbkr," "hukbkr," "hkubkr," "hukubkr," "hkbukr,"... are stored in the index structure.

As for the conversion model, we employed the discriminative Kana-Kanji conversion model by Tokunaga (2011). The basic algorithm is the same except that the Viterbi search also runs on consonant sequences rather than Kana ones. We used surface unigram, surface + class (PoS tags) unigram, surface + reading unigram, class bigram, surface bigram as features. The red lines in Figure 3 illustrate the finally chosen path.

The suggestion candidates, which is to show candidates such as *hukubukuro* (lucky bag) and *hontai* (body) for an input "H," are chosen from 2000 most frequent query fragments issued in 2011 at Rakuten Ichiba[4]. We annotate each query with Kana pronunciation, which is converted into possible consonant sequence as in the previous section. At run-time, prefix search is perfomed on this consonant trie to obtain the candidate list. The candidate list is sorted by the frequency, and shown to the user supplementing the Kana-Kanji conversion results.

4 Experiments

In this section, we compare KooSHO with *Siri* and a software keyboard system. We used the following three training corpora: 1) BCCWJ-CORE (60,374 sentences and 1,286,899 tokens)[5], 2) EC corpus, consists of 1,230 product titles and descriptions randomly sampled from Rakuten Ichiba (118,355 tokens). 3) EC query log (2000 most frequent query fragments issued in 2011 at Rakuten Ichiba) As the dictionary, we used UniDic[6].

Character Recognition Firstly, we evaluate the accuracy of the character recognition model. For each letter from "A" to "Z," two subjects attempted to type the letter for three times, and the accuracy how many times the character was correctly recognized was measured.

We observed recognition accuracy varies from letter to letter. Letters which have similar forms, such as "F" and "T" can be easily misrecognized, leading lower accuracy. For some of the cases where the letter shape completely contains a shape of the other, e.g., "F" and "E," recognition error is inevitable. The overall character recognition accuracy was 0.76.

Kana-Kanji Conversion Secondly, we evaluate the accuracy of the Kana-Kanji conversion algorithm. We used ACC (averaged Top-1 accuracy), MFS (mean F score), and MRR (mean reciprocal rank) as evaluation measures (Li et al., 2009). We used a test set consisting of 100 words and phrases which are randomly extracted from Rakuten Ichiba, popular products and query logs. The result was ACC = 0.24, MFS = 0.50, and MRR = 0.30, which suggests the right choice comes at the top 24 percent of the time, about half (50%) the characters of the top candidate match the answer, and the average position of the answer is 1 / MRR = 3.3. Notice that this is a very strict evaluation since it does not allow partial input. For example, even if "フィットネスシューズ" *fittonesushu-zu* (fitness shoes) does not come up at the top, one could obtain the same result by inputting "フィットネス" (fitness) and "シューズ" (shoes) separately. Also, we found that some spelling variations such as まつげ and まつ毛 (both meaning eyelashes) lower the evaluation result, even though

[3]http://support.microsoft.com/kb/883232/ja
[4]http://www.rakuten.co.jp/
[5]http://www.ninjal.ac.jp/corpus_center/bccwj/
[6]http://www.tokuteicorpus.jp/dist/

they are not a problem in practice.

Overall Evaluation Lastly, we evaluate the overall input accuracy, speed, and user experience comparing *Siri*, a screen keyboard (Tablet PC Input Panel) controlled by Kinect using KinEmote[7], and KooSHO.

First, we measured the recognition accuracy of *Siri* based on the 100 test queries. The accuracy turned out to be 85%, and the queries were recognized within three to four seconds. However, about 14% of the queries cannot be recognized even after many attempts. There are especially two types of queries where voice recognition performed poorly — the first one is relatively new, unknown words such as オーガランド (ogaland), which obviously depends on the recognition system's language models and the vocabulary set. The second the is homonyms, i.e., voice recognition is, in principle, unable to discern multiple words with the same pronunciation, such as "包装" (package) and "放送" (broadcast) *housou*, and "ミョウバン" (alum) and "明晩" (tomorrow evening) *myouban*. This is where KooSHO-like visual feedback on the conversion results has a clear advantage.

Second, we tried the screen keyboard controlled by Kinect. Using a screen keyboard was extremely difficult, almost impossible, since it requires fine movement of hands in order to place the cursor over the desired keys. Therefore, only the time required to place the cursor on the desired keys in order was measured. The fact that users have to type out all the characters including vowels is making the matter worse. This is also where KooSHO excels.

Finally, we measured the time taken for KooSHO to complete each query. The result varied depending on query, but the ones which contain characters with low recognition accuracy such as "C" (e.g., "チーズ" (cheese)) took longer. The average was 35 seconds.

Conclusion and Future Works

In this paper, we proposed a novel environment for Japanese text input based on aerial hand gestures called KooSHO, which provides an integrated experience of character input, Kana-Kanji conversion, and search result visualization. This is the first to propose a Japanese text input system beyond single characters based on hand gestures. The system has several novelties, including 1) non-restrictive character forms, 2) robust continuous recognition and Kana-Kanji conversion, and 3) faster input by suggestions and consonant input. The comparison with voice recognition and a screen keyboard showed KooSHO can be a more practical solution compared to the screen keyboard.

Since KooSHO is an integrated Japanese input environment, not just a character recognition software, many features implemented in modern input methods, such as fuzzy matching and user personalization, can also be implemented. In particular, how to let the user modify the mistaken input is a great challenge.

[7]http://www.kinemote.net/

References

Xinying Han, Hiroaki Seki, Yoshitsugu kamiya, and Masatoshi Hikizu. 2007. Wearable handwriting input device using magnetic field. In *Proc. of SICE*, pages 365–368.

Taku Kudo, Kaoru Yamamoto, and Yuji Matsumoto. 2004. Applying conditional random fields to Japanese morphological analysis. In *Proc. of EMNLP*, pages 230–237.

Haizhou Li, A Kumaran, Vladimir Pervouchine, and Min Zhang. 2009. Report of news 2009 machine transliteration shared task. In *Proc. of NEWS*, pages 1–18.

Tomonari Sonoda and Yoishic Muraoka. 2003. A letter input system of handwriting gesture (in Japanese). *The Transactions of the Institute of Electronics, Information and Communication Engineers D-II*, J86-D-II:1015–1025.

Kumiko Tanaka-Ishii, Yusuke Inutsuka, and Masato Takeichi. 2001. Japanese text input system with digits. In *Proc. of HLT*, pages 1–8.

Hiroyuki Tokunaga, Daisuke Okanohara, and Shinsuke Mori. 2011. Discriminative method for Japanese kana-kanji input method. In *Proc. of WTIM*.

Ho-Sub Yoon, Jung Soh, Byung-Woo Min, and Hyun Seung Yang. 1999. Recognition of alphabetical hand gestures using hidden markov model. *IEICE Trans. Fundamentals*, E82-A(7):1358–1366.

UMLS::Similarity: Measuring the Relatedness and Similarity of Biomedical Concepts

Bridget T. McInnes* **& Ying Liu**
Minnesota Supercomputing Institute
University of Minnesota
Minneapolis, MN 55455

Ted Pedersen
Department of Computer Science
University of Minnesota
Duluth, MN 55812

Genevieve B. Melton
Institute for Health Informatics
University of Minnesota
Minneapolis, MN 55455

Serguei V. Pakhomov
College of Pharmacy
University of Minnesota
Minneapolis, MN 55455

Abstract

UMLS::Similarity is freely available open source software that allows a user to measure the semantic similarity or relatedness of biomedical terms found in the Unified Medical Language System (UMLS). It is written in Perl and can be used via a command line interface, an API, or a Web interface.

1 Introduction

UMLS::Similarity[1] implements a number of semantic similarity and relatedness measures that are based on the structure and content of the Unified Medical Language System. The UMLS is a data warehouse that provides a unified view of many medical terminologies, ontologies and other lexical resources, and is also freely available from the National Library of Medicine.[2]

Measures of semantic similarity quantify the degree to which two terms are similar based on their proximity in an *is-a* hierarchy. These measures are often based on the distance between the two concepts and their common ancestor. For example, *lung disease* and *Goodpasture's Syndrome* share the concept *disease* as a common ancestor. Or in general English, *scalpel* and *switchblade* would be considered very similar since both are nearby descendents of the concept *knife*.

However, concepts that are not technically similar can still be very closely related. For example, *Goodpasture's Syndrome* and *Doxycycline* are not similar since they do not have a nearby common ancestor, but they are very closely related since *Doxycycline* is a possible treatment for *Goodpasture's Syndrome*. A more general example might be *elbow* and *arm*, while they are not similar, an *elbow* is a *part-of* an *arm* and is therefore very closely related. Measures of relatedness quantify these types of relationships by using information beyond that which is found in an *is-a hierarchy*, which the UMLS contains in abundance.

2 Related Work

Measures of semantic similarity and relatedness have been used in a number of different biomedical and clinical applications. Early work relied on the Gene Ontology (GO)[3], which is a hierarchy of terms used to describe genomic information. For example, (Lord et al., 2003) measured the similarity of gene sequence data and used this in an application for conducting semantic searches of textual resources. (Guo et al., 2006) used semantic similarity measures to identify direct and indirect protein interactions within human regulatory pathways. (Névéol et al., 2006) used semantic similarity measures based on MeSH (Medical Subject Headings)[4] to evaluate automatic indexing of biomedical articles by measuring the similarity between their recommended terms and the gold standard index terms.

UMLS::Similarity was first released in 2009, and since that time has been used in various different applications. (Sahay and Ram, 2010) used it in a

*Contact author : bthomson@umn.edu.

[1] http://umls-similarity.sourceforge.net

[2] http://www.nlm.nih.gov/research/umls/

[3] http://www.geneontology.org/

[4] http://www.ncbi.nlm.nih.gov/mesh

health information search and recommendation system. (Zhang et al., 2011) used the measures to identify redundancy within clinical records, while (Mathur and Dinakarpandian, 2011) used them to help identify similar diseases. UMLS::Similarity has also enabled the development and evaluation of new measures by allowing them to be compared to existing methods, e.g., (Pivovarov and Elhadad, 2012). Finally, UMLS::Similarity can serve as a building block in other NLP systems, for example UMLS::SenseRelate (McInnes et al., 2011) is a word sense disambiguation system for medical text based on semantic similarity and relatedness.

Table 1: UMLS::Similarity Measures

Type	Citation	Name
Similarity	(Rada et al., 1989)	path
	(Caviedes and Cimino, 2004)	cdist
	(Wu and Palmer, 1994)	wup
	(Leacock and Chodorow, 1998)	lch
	(Nguyen and Al-Mubaid, 2006)	nam
	(Zhong et al., 2002)	zhong
	(Resnik, 1995)	res
	(Lin, 1998)	lin
	(Jiang and Conrath, 1997)	jcn
Relatedness	(Banerjee and Pedersen, 2003)	lesk
	(Patwardhan and Pedersen, 2006)	vector

3 UMLS::Similarity

UMLS::Similarity is a descendent of WordNet::Similarity (Pedersen et al., 2004), which implements various measures of similarity and relatedness for WordNet.[5] However, the structure, nature, and size of the UMLS is quite different from WordNet, and the adaptations from WordNet were not always straightforward. One very significant difference, for example, is that the UMLS is stored in a MySQL database while WordNet has its own customized storage format. As a result, the core of UMLS::Similarity is different and offers a great deal of functionality specific to the UMLS. Table 1 lists the measures currently provided in UMLS::Similarity (as of version 1.27).

The Web interface provides a subset of the functionality offered by the API and command line interface, and allows a user to utilize UMLS::Similarity without requiring the installation of the UMLS (which is an admittedly time–consuming process).

4 Unified Medical Language System

The UMLS is a data warehouse that includes over 100 different biomedical and clinical data resources. One of the largest individual sources is the Systematized Nomenclature of Medicine–Clinical Terms (SNOMED CT), a comprehensive terminology created for the electronic exchange of clinical health information. Perhaps the most fine–grained source is the Foundational Model of Anatomy (FMA), an ontology created for biomedical and clinical research. One of the most popular sources is MeSH (MSH), a terminology that is used for indexing medical journal articles in PubMed.

These many different resources are semi-automatically combined into the Metathesaurus, which provides a unified view of nearly 3,000,000 different concepts. This is very important since the same concept can exist in multiple different sources. For example, the concept *Autonomic nerve* exists in both SNOMED CT and FMA. The Metathesaurus assigns synonymous concepts from multiple sources a single Concept Unique Identifier (CUI). Thus both *Autonomic nerve* concepts in SNOMED CT and FMA are assigned the same CUI (C0206250). These shared CUIs essentially merge multiple sources into a single resource in the Metathesaurus.

Some sources in the Metathesaurus contain additional information about the concept such as synonyms, definitions,[6] and related concepts. Parent/child (PAR/CHD) and broader/narrower (RB/RN) are the main types of hierarchical relations between concepts in the Metathesaurus. Parent/child relations are already defined in the sources before they are integrated into the UMLS, whereas broader/-narrower relations are added by the UMLS editors. For example, *Splanchnic nerve* has an *is-a* relation with *Autonomic nerve* in FMA. This relation is carried forward in the Metathesaurus by creating a parent/child relation between the CUIs C0037991 [Splanchnic nerve] and C0206250 [Autonomic nerve].

[5]http://wordnet.princeton.edu/

[6]However, not all concepts in the UMLS have a definition.

Table 2: Similarity scores for *finger* and *arm*

Source	Relations	CUIs	path	cdist	wup	lch	nam	zhong	res	lin	jcn
FMA	PAR/CHD	82,071	0.14	0.14	0.69	1.84	0.15	0.06	0.82	0.34	0.35
SNOMED CT	PAR/CHD	321,357	0.20	0.20	0.73	2.45	0.15	0.16	2.16	0.62	0.48
MSH	PAR/CHD	26,685	0.25	0.25	0.76	2.30	0.18	0.19	2.03	0.68	0.55

5 Demonstration System

The UMLS::Similarity Web interface[7] allows a user to enter two terms or UMLS CUIs as input in term boxes. The user can choose to calculate similarity or relatedness by clicking on the **Calculate Similarity** or **Calculate Relatedness** button. The user can also choose which UMLS sources and relations should be used in the calculation. For example, if the terms *finger* and *arm* are entered and the **Compute Similarity** button is pressed, the following is output:

```
View Definitions
View Shortest Path

Results:
The similarity of finger
(C0016129) and arm (C0446516)
using Path Length (path) is
0.25.

Using:
  SAB :: include MSH
  REL :: include PAR/CHD
```

The **Results** show the terms and their assigned CUIs. If a term has multiple possible CUIs associated with it, UMLS::Similarity returns the CUI pair that obtained the highest similarity score. In this case, *finger* was assigned CUI *C0016129* and *arm* assigned CUI *C0449516* and the resulting similarity score for the path measure using the MeSH hierarchy was 0.25.

Additionally, the paths between the concepts and their definitions are shown. The **View Definitions** and **View Shortest Path** buttons show the definition and shortest path between the concepts in a separate window. In the example above, the shortest path between *finger* (C0016129) and *arm* (C0446516) is **C0016129 (Finger, NOS) => C0018563 (Hand, NOS) => C1140618 (Extremity, Upper) => C0446516 (Upper arm)**, and one of the definitions shown for *arm* (C0446516) is **The superior part of the upper extremity between the shoulder and the elbow.**

SAB :: **include** and **REL** :: **include** are configuration parameters that define the sources and relations used to find the paths between the two CUIs when measuring similarity. In the example above, similarity was calculated using PAR/CHD relations in the MeSH hierarchy.

All similarity measures default to the use of MeSH as the source (SAB) with PAR/CHD relations. While these are reasonable defaults, for many use cases these should be changed. Table 2 shows the similarity scores returned for each measure using different sources. It also shows the number of CUIs connected via PAR/CHD relations per source.

A similar view is displayed when pressing the **Compute Relatedness** button:

```
View Definitions
View Shortest Path

Results:
The relatedness of finger
(C0016129) and arm (C0446516)
using Vector Measure (vector)
is 0.5513.

Using:
  SABDEF :: include
       UMLS_ALL
  RELDEF :: include
       CUI/PAR/CHD/RB/RN
```

Relatedness measures differ from similarity in their use of the SABDEF and RELDEF parameters. **SABDEF** :: **include** and **RELDEF** :: **include** define the source(s) and relation(s) used to extract definitions for the relatedness measures. In this example, the definitions come from any source in the UMLS and include not only the definition of the concept but

[7] http://atlas.ahc.umn.edu/

Table 3: Relatedness scores for *finger* and *arm*

Source	Relations	lesk	vector
UMLS_ALL	CUI/PAR/CHD/RB/RN	10,607	0.55
UMLS_ALL	CUI	39	0.05

also the definition of its PAR/CHD and RB/RN relations. Table 3 shows the relatedness scores returned for each of the relatedness measures using just the concept's definition (CUI) from all of the sources in the UMLS (UMLS_ALL) and when the definitions are extended to include the definitions of the concept's PAR/CHD and RB/RN relations.

6 Acknowledgments

This work was supported by the National Institute of Health, National Library of Medicine Grant #R01LM009623-01. It was carried out in part using computing resources at the University of Minnesota Supercomputing Institute.

The results reported here are based on the 2012AA version of the UMLS and were computed using version 1.23 of UMLS::Similarity and version 1.27 of UMLS::Interface.

References

S. Banerjee and T. Pedersen. 2003. Extended gloss overlaps as a measure of semantic relatedness. In *Proceedings of the Eighteenth International Joint Conference on Artificial Intelligence*, pages 805–810, Acapulco, August.

J.E. Caviedes and J.J. Cimino. 2004. Towards the development of a conceptual distance metric for the umls. *Journal of Biomedical Informatics*, 37(2):77–85.

X. Guo, R. Liu, C.D. Shriver, H. Hu, and M.N. Liebman. 2006. Assessing semantic similarity measures for the characterization of human regulatory pathways. *Bioinformatics*, 22(8):967–973.

J. Jiang and D. Conrath. 1997. Semantic similarity based on corpus statistics and lexical taxonomy. In *Proceedings on Intl Conf on Research in CL*, pages pp. 19–33.

C. Leacock and M. Chodorow. 1998. Combining local context and WordNet similarity for word sense identification. *WordNet: An electronic lexical database*, 49(2):265–283.

D. Lin. 1998. An information-theoretic definition of similarity. In *Intl Conf ML Proc.*, pages 296–304.

PW Lord, RD Stevens, A. Brass, and CA Goble. 2003. Semantic similarity measures as tools for exploring the gene ontology. In *Pacific Symposium on Biocomputing*, volume 8, pages 601–612.

S. Mathur and D. Dinakarpandian. 2011. Finding disease similarity based on implicit semantic similarity. *Journal of Biomedical Informatics*, 45(2):363–371.

B.T. McInnes, T. Pedersen, Y. Liu, S. Pakhomov, and G. Melton. 2011. Knowledge-based method for determining the meaning of ambiguous biomedical terms using information content measures of similarity. In *Proceedings of the Annual Symposium of the American Medical Informatics Association*, pages 895 – 904, Washington, DC.

A. Névéol, K. Zeng, and O. Bodenreider. 2006. Besides Precision & Recall: Exploring Alternative Approaches to Evaluating an Automatic Indexing Tool for MEDLINE. In *AMIA Annu Symp Proc.*, page 589.

H.A. Nguyen and H. Al-Mubaid. 2006. New ontology-based semantic similarity measure for the biomedical domain. In *Proc of the IEEE Intl Conf on Granular Computing*, pages 623–628.

S. Patwardhan and T. Pedersen. 2006. Using WordNet-based Context Vectors to Estimate the Semantic Relatedness of Concepts. In *Proc of the EACL 2006 Workshop Making Sense of Sense*, pages 1–8.

T. Pedersen, S. Patwardhan, and J. Michelizzi. 2004. WordNet::Similarity - Measuring the Relatedness of Concepts. In *The Annual Meeting of the HLT and NAACL: Demonstration Papers*, pages 38–41.

R. Pivovarov and N. Elhadad. 2012. A hybrid knowledge-based and data-driven approach to identifying semantically similar concepts. *Journal of Biomedical Informatics*, 45(3):471–481.

R. Rada, H. Mili, E. Bicknell, and M. Blettner. 1989. Development and application of a metric on semantic nets. *IEEE Transactions on Systems, Man, and Cybernetics*, 19(1):17–30.

P. Resnik. 1995. Using information content to evaluate semantic similarity in a taxonomy. In *Proceedings of the 14th Intl Joint Conf on AI*, pages 448–453.

S. Sahay and A. Ram. 2010. Socio-semantic health information access. In *Proceedings of the AAAI Spring Symposium on AI and Health Communication*.

Z. Wu and M. Palmer. 1994. Verbs semantics and lexical selection. In *Proceedings of the 32nd Meeting of ACL*, pages 133–138, Las Cruces, NM, June.

R. Zhang, S. Pakhomov, B.T. McInnes, and G.B. Melton. 2011. Evaluating measures of redundancy in clinical texts. In *AMIA Annual Symposium Proceedings*, volume 2011, page 1612.

J. Zhong, H. Zhu, J. Li, and Y. Yu. 2002. Conceptual graph matching for semantic search. *Proceedings of the 10th International Conference on Conceptual Structures*, pages 92–106.

KELVIN: a tool for automated knowledge base construction

Paul McNamee, James Mayfield
Johns Hopkins University
Human Language Technology Center of Excellence

Tim Finin, Tim Oates
University of Maryland
Baltimore County

Dawn Lawrie
Loyola University Maryland

Tan Xu, Douglas W. Oard
University of Maryland
College Park

Abstract

We present KELVIN, an automated system for processing a large text corpus and distilling a knowledge base about persons, organizations, and locations. We have tested the KELVIN system on several corpora, including: (a) the TAC KBP 2012 Cold Start corpus which consists of public Web pages from the University of Pennsylvania, and (b) a subset of 26k news articles taken from English Gigaword 5th edition.

Our NAACL HLT 2013 demonstration permits a user to interact with a set of searchable HTML pages, which are automatically generated from the knowledge base. Each page contains information analogous to the semi-structured details about an entity that are present in Wikipedia Infoboxes, along with hyperlink citations to supporting text.

1 Introduction

The Text Analysis Conference (TAC) Knowledge Base Population (KBP) Cold Start task[1] requires systems to take set of documents and produce a comprehensive set of <Subject, Predicate, Object> triples that encode relationships between and attributes of the named-entities that are mentioned in the corpus. Systems are evaluated based on the fidelity of the constructed knowledge base. For the 2012 evaluation, a fixed schema of 42 relations (or slots), and their logical inverses was provided, for example:

- X:Organization employs Y:Person
- X:Person has-job-title *title*
- X:Organization headquartered-in Y:Location

Multiple layers of NLP software are required for this undertaking, including at the least: detection of named-entities, intra-document co-reference resolution, relation extraction, and entity disambiguation.

To help prevent a bias towards learning about prominent entities at the expense of generality, KELVIN refrains from mining facts from sources such as documents obtained through Web search, Wikipedia[2], or DBpedia.[3] Only facts that are asserted in and gleaned from the source documents are posited.

Other systems that create large-scale knowledge bases from general text include the Never-Ending Language Learning (NELL) system at Carnegie Mellon University (Carlson et al., 2010), and the TextRunner system developed at the University of Washington (Etzioni et al., 2008).

2 Washington Post KB

No gold-standard KBs were available to us to assist during the development of KELVIN, so we relied on qualitative assessment to gauge the effectiveness of our extracted relations – by manually examining ten random samples for each relations, we ascertained that most relations were between 30-80% accurate. Although the TAC KBP 2012 Cold Start task was a pilot evaluation of a new task using a novel evaluation methodology, the KELVIN system did attain the highest reported F_1 scores.[4]

[1] See details at `http://www.nist.gov/tac/2012/KBP/task_guidelines/index.html`

[2] `http://en.wikipedia.org/`

[3] `http://www.dbpedia.org/`

[4] 0.497 0-hop & 0.363 all-hops, as reported in the preliminary TAC 2012 Evaluation Results.

During our initial development we worked with a 26,143 document collection of 2010 Washington Post articles and the system discovered 194,059 relations about 57,847 named entities. KELVIN learns some interesting, but rather dubious relations from the Washington Post articles[5]

- Sen. Harry Reid is an employee of the "Republican Party." Sen. Reid is also an employee of the "Democratic Party."
- Big Foot is an employee of Starbucks.
- MacBook Air is a subsidiary of Apple Inc.
- Jill Biden is married to Jill Biden.

However, KELVIN also learns quite a number of correct facts, including:

- Warren Buffett owns shares of Berkshire Hathaway, Burlington Northern Santa Fe, the Washington Post Co., and four other stocks.
- Jared Fogle is an employee of Subway.
- Freeman Hrabowski works for UMBC, founded the Meyerhoff Scholars Program, and graduated from Hampton University and the University of Illinois.
- Supreme Court Justice Elena Kagan attended Oxford, Harvard, and Princeton.
- Southwest Airlines is headquartered in Texas.
- Ian Soboroff is a computer scientist[6] employed by NIST.[7]

3 Pipeline Components

3.1 SERIF

BBN's SERIF tool[8] (Boschee et al., 2005) provides a considerable suite of document annotations that are an excellent basis for building a knowledge base. The functions SERIF can provide are based largely on the NIST ACE specification,[9] and include: (a) identifying named-entities and classifying them by type and subtype; (b) performing intra-document co-reference analysis, including named mentions, as well as co-referential nominal and pronominal mentions; (c) parsing sentences and extracting intra-sentential relations between entities; and, (d) detecting certain types of events.

Slotname	*Count*
per:employee_of	60,690
org:employees	44,663
gpe:employees	16,027
per:member_of	14,613
org:membership	14,613
org:city_of_headquarters	12,598
gpe:headquarters_in_city	12,598
org:parents	6,526
org:country_of_headquarters	4,503
gpe:headquarters_in_country	4,503

Table 1: Most prevalent slots extracted by SERIF from the Washington Post texts.

Slotname	*Count*
per:title	44,896
per:employee_of	39,101
per:member_of	20,735
per:countries_of_residence	8,192
per:origin	4,187
per:statesorprovinces_of_residence	3,376
per:cities_of_residence	3,376
per:country_of_birth	1,577
per:age	1,233
per:spouse	1,057

Table 2: Most prevalent slots extracted by FACETS from the Washington Post texts.

In Table 1 we list the most common slots SERIF extracts from the Washington Post articles.

3.2 FACETS

FACETS, another BBN tool, is an add-on package that takes SERIF output and produces role and argument annotations about person noun phrases. FACETS is implemented using a conditional-

[5]All 2010 Washington Post articles from English Gigaword 5th ed. (LDC2011T07).

[6]Ian is the sole computer scientist discovered in processing a year of news. In contrast, KELVIN found 52 lobbyists.

[7]From Washington Post article (WPB_ENG_20100506.0012 in LDC2011T07).

[8]Statistical Entity & Relation Information Finding.

[9]The principal types of ACE named-entities are persons, organizations, and geo-political entities (GPEs). GPEs are inhabited locations with a government. See http://www.itl.nist.gov/iad/mig/tests/ace/2008/doc/ace08-evalplan.v1.2d.pdf.

```
:e_WPB_ENG_20100112_0031_13 is "Joe Scarborough"
:e_WPB_ENG_20100112_0031_13 "Joe Scarborough" per:employee_of WPB_ENG_20100112.0031 :e_WPB_ENG_20100914_0057_24 "Nevada"
:e_WPB_ENG_20100112_0031_13 "Joe Scarborough" per:employee_of WPB_ENG_20100112.0031 :e_WPB_ENG_20100713_0046_6 "The Washington Post"
:e_WPB_ENG_20100112_0031_13 "Joe Scarborough" per:employee_of WPB_ENG_20101119.0056 :e_WPB_ENG_20100205_0049_41 "Florida"
:e_WPB_ENG_20100112_0031_13 "Joe Scarborough" per:employee_of WPB_ENG_20101205.0014 :e_WPB_ENG_20100822_0012_16 "MSNBC"
:e_WPB_ENG_20100112_0031_13 "Joe Scarborough" per:employee_of WPB_ENG_20101205.0014 :e_WPB_ENG_20101021_0024_12 "Alaska"
:e_WPB_ENG_20100112_0031_13 "Joe Scarborough" per:member_of WPB_ENG_20100703.0014 :e_WPB_ENG_20100609_0026_3 "Republican House"
:e_WPB_ENG_20100112_0031_13 "Joe Scarborough" per:member_of WPB_ENG_20100707.0009 :e_WPB_ENG_20100521_0034_18 "Republican National Committee"
:e_WPB_ENG_20100112_0031_13 "Joe Scarborough" per:member_of WPB_ENG_20101204.0003 :e_WPB_ENG_20100122_0067_2 "Republican"
:e_WPB_ENG_20100112_0031_13 "Joe Scarborough" per:member_of WPB_ENG_20101205.0014 :e_WPB_ENG_20100809_0034_8 "Republican Party"
:e_WPB_ENG_20100112_0031_13 "Joe Scarborough" per:siblings WPB_ENG_20101119.0091 :e_WPB_ENG_20101119_0091_7 "George Scarborough"
:e_WPB_ENG_20100112_0031_13 "Joe Scarborough" per:statesorprovinces_of_residence WPB_ENG_20101205.0014 :e_WPB_ENG_20100205_0049_41 "Florida"
:e_WPB_ENG_20100112_0031_13 "Joe Scarborough" per:title WPB_ENG_20101119.0056 "congressman" NIL
```

Figure 1: Simple rendering of KB page about former Florida congressman Joe Scarborough. Many facts are correct – he lived in and was employed by the State of Florida; he has a brother George; he was a member of the Republican House of Representatives; and, he is employed by MSNBC.

exponential learner trained on broadcast news. The attributes FACETS can recognize include general attributes like religion and age (which anyone might have), as well as role-specific attributes, such as medical specialty for physicians, or academic institution for someone associated with an university.

In Table 2 we report the most prevalent slots FACETS extracts from the Washington Post.[10]

3.3 CUNY toolkit

To increase our coverage of relations we also integrated the KBP Slot Filling Toolkit (Chen et al., 2011) developed at the CUNY BLENDER Lab. Given that the KBP toolkit was designed for the traditional slot filling task at TAC, this primarily involved creating the queries that the tool expected as input and parallelizing the toolkit to handle the vast number of queries issued in the cold start scenarios.

To informally gauge the accuracy of slots extracted from the CUNY tool, some coarse assessment was done over a small collection of 807 New York Times articles that include the string "University of Kansas." From this collection, 4264 slots were identified. Nine different types of slots were filled in order of frequency: per:title (37%), per:employee_of (23%), per:cities_of_residence (17%), per:stateorprovinces_of_residence (6%), org:top_members/employees (6%), org:member_of (6%), per:countries_of_residence (2%), per:spouse (2%), and per:member_of (1%). We randomly sampled 10 slot-fills of each type, and found accuracy to vary from 20-70%.

[10]Note FACETS can independently extract some slots that SERIF is capable of discovering (*e.g.*, employment relations).

3.4 Coreference

We used two methods for entity coreference. Under the theory that name ambiguity may not be a huge problem, we adopted a baseline approach of merging entities across different documents if their canonical mentions were an exact string match after some basic normalizations, such as removing punctuation and conversion to lower-case characters. However we also used the JHU HLTCOE CALE system (Stoyanov et al., 2012), which maps named-entity mentions to the TAC-KBP reference KB, which was derived from a 2008 snapshot of English Wikipedia. For entities that are not found in the KB, we reverted to exact string match. CALE entity linking proved to be the more effective approach for the Cold Start task.

3.5 Timex2 Normalization

SERIF recognizes, but does not normalize, temporal expressions, so we used the Stanford SUTime package, to normalize date values.

```
Scarborough confessed to violating the rule after Politico.com turned up five
contributions of $500 each, and MSNBC found three more that he'd made to
candidates in local races in Florida over the past four years.
</P>
<P>
Among others, Scarborough contributed to his brother, George Scarborough, who
ran unsuccessfully for a seat in Florida's legislature in 2007, and to a
candidate who had served as Scarborough's chief of staff in Washington when
Scarborough was a Republican congressman from Florida.
</P>
```

Figure 2: Supporting text for some assertions about Mr. Scarborough. Source documents are also viewable by following hyperlinks.

3.6 Lightweight Inference

We performed a small amount of light inference to fill some slots. For example, if we identified that a person P worked for organization O, and we also extracted a job title T for P, and if T matched a set of titles such as *president* or *minister* we asserted that the tuple <O, org:top_members_employees, P> relation also held.

4 Ongoing Work

There are a number of improvements that we are undertaking, including: scaling to much larger corpora, detecting contradictions, expanding the use of inference, exploiting the confidence of extracted information, and applying KELVIN to various genres of text.

5 Script Outline

The KB generated by KELVIN is best explored using a Wikipedia metaphor. Thus our demonstration consists of a web browser that starts with a list of moderately prominent named-entities that the user can choose to examine (*e.g.,* investor Warren Buffett, Supreme Court Justice Elena Kagan, Southwest Airlines Co., the state of Florida). Selecting any entity takes one to a page displaying its known attributes and relations, with links to documents that serve as provenance for each assertion. On every page, each entity is hyperlinked to its own canonical page; therefore the user is able to browse the KB much as one browses Wikipedia by simply following links. A sample generated page is shown in Figure 1 and text that supports some of the learned assertions in the figure is shown in Figure 2. We also provide a search interface to support jumping to a desired entity and can demonstrate accessing the data encoded in the semantic web language RDF (World Wide Web Consortium, 2013), which supports ontology browsing and executing complex SPARQL queries (Prud'Hommeaux and Seaborne, 2008) such as "List the employers of people living in Nebraska or Kansas who are older than 40."

References

E. Boschee, R. Weischedel, and A. Zamanian. 2005. Automatic information extraction. In *Proceedings of the 2005 International Conference on Intelligence Analysis, McLean, VA*, pages 2–4.

Andrew Carlson, Justin Betteridge, Bryan Kisiel, Burr Settles, Estevam R. Hruschka Jr., and Tom M. Mitchell. 2010. Toward an architecture for never-ending language learning. In *Proceedings of the Twenty-Fourth Conference on Artificial Intelligence (AAAI 2010)*.

Z. Chen, S. Tamang, A. Lee, X. Li, and H. Ji. 2011. Knowledge Base Population (KBP) Toolkit @ CUNY BLENDER LAB Manual.

Oren Etzioni, Michele Banko, Stephen Soderland, and Daniel S. Weld. 2008. Open information extraction from the web. *Commun. ACM*, 51(12):68–74, December.

E Prud'Hommeaux and A. Seaborne. 2008. SPARQL query language for RDF. Technical report, World Wide Web Consortium, January.

Veselin Stoyanov, James Mayfield, Tan Xu, Douglas W. Oard, Dawn Lawrie, Tim Oates, and Tim Finin. 2012. A context-aware approach to entity linking. In *Proceedings of the Joint Workshop on Automatic Knowledge Base Construction and Web-scale Knowledge Extraction*, AKBC-WEKEX '12, pages 62–67, Stroudsburg, PA, USA. Association for Computational Linguistics.

World Wide Web Consortium. 2013. Resource Description Framework Specification. "`http://http://www.w3.org/RDF/.` "[Online; accessed 8 April, 2013]".

Argviz: Interactive Visualization of Topic Dynamics in Multi-party Conversations

Viet-An Nguyen
Dept. of Comp. Science and UMIACS
University of Maryland
College Park, MD
vietan@cs.umd.edu

Yuening Hu
Dept. of Comp. Science and UMIACS
University of Maryland
College Park, MD
ynhu@cs.umd.edu

Jordan Boyd-Graber
iSchool and UMIACS
University of Maryland
College Park, MD
jbg@umiacs.umd.edu

Philip Resnik
Department of Linguistics and UMIACS
University of Maryland
College Park, MD
resnik@umd.edu

Abstract

We introduce an efficient, interactive framework—*Argviz*—for experts to analyze the dynamic topical structure of multi-party conversations. Users inject their needs, expertise, and insights into models via iterative topic refinement. The refined topics feed into a segmentation model, whose outputs are shown to users via multiple coordinated views.

1 Introduction

Uncovering the structure of conversations often requires close reading by a human expert to be effective. Political debates are an interesting example: political scientists carefully analyze what gets said in debates to explore how candidates shape the debate's agenda and frame issues or how answers subtly (or not so subtly) shift the conversation by dodging the question that was asked (Rogers and Norton, 2011).

Computational methods can contribute to the analysis of topical dynamics, for example through topic segmentation, dividing a conversation into smaller, topically coherent segments (Purver, 2011); or through identifying and summarizing the topics under discussion (Blei et al., 2003; Blei, 2012). However, the topics uncovered by such methods can be difficult for people to interpret (Chang et al., 2009), and previous visualization frameworks for topic models—e.g., ParallelTopics (Dou et al., 2011), TopicViz (Eisenstein et al., 2012), the Topical Guide,[1] or topic model visualization (Chaney and Blei, 2012)—are not particularly well suited for linearly structured *conversations*.

This paper describes *Argviz,* an integrated, interactive system for analyzing the topical dynamics of multi-party conversations. We bring together previous work on *Interactive Topic Modeling* (ITM) (Hu et al., 2011), which allows users to efficiently inject their needs, expertise, and insights into model building via iterative topic refinement, with *Speaker Identity for Topic Segmentation* (SITS) (Nguyen et al., 2012), a state-of-the-art model for topic segmentation and discovery of topic shifts in conversations. *Argviz*'s interface allows users to quickly grasp the topical flow of the conversation, discern when the topic changes and by whom, and interactively visualize the conversation's details on demand.

[1] `http://tg.byu.edu/`

2 System Overview

Our overall system consists of three steps: (1) data preprocessing, (2) interactive topic modeling, and (3) conversational topic segmentation and visualization.

Data preprocessing Preprocessing creates bags of words that can be used by models. First, stopwords and low frequency terms are removed from tokenized text. This is then used as the data for topic modeling.

Interactive topic modeling The topic modeling process then discovers—through posterior inference—the topics that best explain the conversational turns. Each of the topics is a multinomial distribution over words, which can be displayed to users along with the association of turns (documents) to these topics.

The result of topic modeling may be imperfect; we give users an opportunity to refine and curate the topics using Interactive Topic Modeling (ITM) (Hu et al., 2011). The feedback from users is encoded in the form of **correlations**: word types that should co-occur in a topic or which should not. As these correlations are incorporated into the model, the topics learned by the model change and are presented again to the user. The process repeats over multiple iterations until the user is satisfied.

In addition, a simple but important part of the interactive user experience is the ability for users to **label** topics, i.e., to identify a "congress" topic that includes "bill", "vote", "representative", etc.

ITM is a web-based application with a HTML and jQuery[2] front end, connected via Ajax and JSON.

Topic segmentation After the user has built interpretable topics, we use SITS—a hierarchical topic model (Nguyen et al., 2012)—to jointly discover the set of topics discussed in a given set of conversations and how these topics change during each conversation. We use the output of ITM to initialize SITS[3] with a high quality user-specific set of topics. The outputs of SITS consist of (1) a set of topics, (2) a distribution over topics for each turn, and (3) a probability associated with each turn indicating how likely the topic of that turn has been shifted.

The outputs of SITS are displayed using *Argviz* (Figure 2). *Argviz* is a web-based application, built using Google Web Toolkit (GWT),[4] which allows users to visualize and manipulate SITS's outputs entirely in their browser after a single server request.

3 *Argviz:* Coordinated Conversational Views

Given the limited screen of a web browser, *Argviz* follows the multiple coordinated views approach (Wang Baldonado et al., 2000; North and Shneiderman, 2000) successfully used in Spotfire (Ahlberg, 1996), Improvise (Weaver, 2004), and SocialAction (Perer and Shneiderman, 2006). *Argviz* supports three main coordinated views: *transcript*, *overview* and *topic*.

Transcript occupies the prime real estate for a close reading. It has a *transcript panel* and a *speaker panel*. The *transcript panel* displays the original transcript. Each conversational turn is numbered and color-coded by speaker. The color associated with each speaker can be customized using the *speaker panel*, which lists all the speakers.

[2] http://jquery.com/

[3] Through per-word topic assignments

[4] https://developers.google.com/web-toolkit/

Overview shows how topics gain and lose prominence during the conversation. SITS's outputs include a topic distribution and a topic shift probability for each turn in the conversation. In *Argviz,* these are represented using a *heatmap* and *topic shift column*.

In the *heatmap*, each turn-specific topic distribution is displayed by a heatmap row (Sopan et al., 2013). There is a cell for each topic, and the color intensity of each cell is proportional to the probability of the corresponding topic of a particular turn. Thus, users can see the topical flow of the conversation through the vertical change in cells' color intensities as the conversation progresses. In addition, the *topic shift column* shows the topic shift probability (inferred by SITS) using color-coded bar charts, helping users discern large topic changes in the conversation. Each row is associated with a turn in the conversation; clicking on one shifts the *transcript view*.

Topic displays the set of topics learned by SITS (primed by ITM), with font-size proportional to the words' topic probabilities. The *selected topic panel* goes into more detail, with bar charts showing the topic-word distribution. For example, in Figure 2, the Foreign Affairs topic in panel E has high probability words "iraq", "afghanistan", "war", etc. in panel F.

4 Demo: Detecting 2008 Debate Dodges

Visitors will have the opportunity to experiment with the process of analyzing the topical dynamics of different multi-party conversations. Multiple datasets will be preprocessed and set up for users to choose and analyze. Examples of datasets that will be available include conversation transcripts from CNN's *Crossfire* program and debates from the 2008 and 2012 U.S. presidential campaigns. For this section, we focus on examples from the 2008 campaign.

Interactive topic refinement After selecting a dataset and a number of topics, the first thing a user can do is to label topics. This will be used later in *Argviz* and helps users build a mental model of what the topics are. For instance, the user may rename the second topic "Foreign Policy".

After inspecting the "Foreign Policy" topic, the user may notice the omission of Iran from the most probable words in the topic. A user can remedy that by adding the words "Iran" and "Iranians" into the

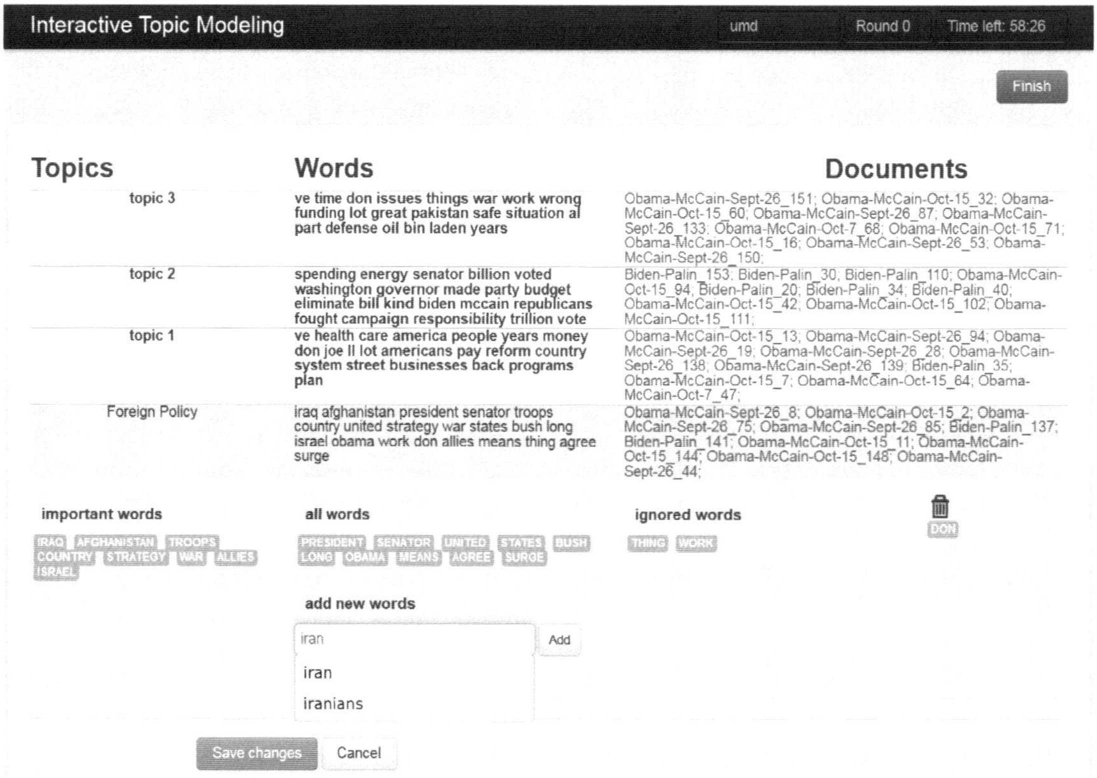

Figure 1: ITM user interface for refining a topic. Users can iteratively put words into different "bins", label topics, and add new words to the topic. Users can also click on the provided links to show related turns for each topic in context.

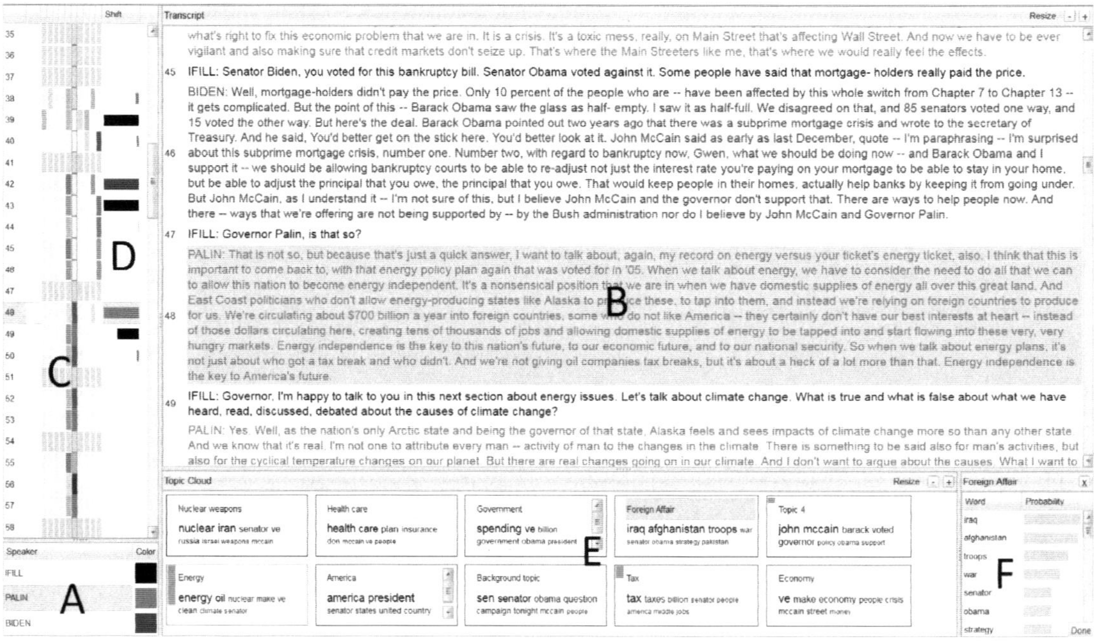

Figure 2: The *Argviz* user interface consists of *speaker panel* (A), *transcript panel* (B), *heatmap* (C), *topic shift column* (D), *topic cloud panel* (E), *selected topic panel* (F).

important words bin (Figure 1). Other bins include *ignored words* for words that should be removed (e.g., "thing" and "work" from this topic) from the topic and *trash* (e.g., "don", which is a stop word).

The user can commit these changes by pressing the *Save changes* button. The back end relearns given the user's feedback. Once users are satisfied with the topic quality, they can click on the *Finish* button to stop updating topics and start running the SITS model, initialized using the final set of refined topics.

Visual analytic of conversations After SITS finishes (which takes just a few moments), users see the dataset's conversations in the *Argviz* interface. Figure 2 shows *Argviz* displaying the 2008 vice presidential debate between Senator Joe Biden and Governor Sarah Palin, moderated by Gwen Ifill.

Users can start exploring the interface from any of the views described in Section 3 to gain insight about the conversation. For example, a user may be interested in seeing how the "Economy" is discussed in the debates. Clicking on a topic in the *topic cloud panel* highlights that column in the *heatmap*. The user can now see where the "Economy" topic is discussed in the debate. Next to the heatmap, the *topic shift column* when debate participants changed the topic. The red bar in turn 48 shows an interaction where Governor Palin dodged a question on the "bankruptcy bill" to discuss her "record on energy". Clicking on this turn shows the interaction in the *transcript view*, allowing a closer reading.

Users might also want to contrast the topics that were discussed before and after the shift. This can be easily done with the coordination between the *heatmap* and the *topic cloud panel*. Clicking on a cell in the *heatmap* will select the corresponding topic to display in the *selected topic panel*. In our example, the topic of the conversation was shifted from "Economy" to "Energy" at turn 48.

5 Conclusion

Argviz is an efficient, interactive framework that allows experts to analyze the dynamic topical structure of multi-party conversations. We are engaged in collaborations with domain experts in political science exploring the application of this framework to political debates, and collaborators in social psychology exploring the analysis of intra- and inter-cultural negotiation dialogues.

References

[Ahlberg, 1996] Ahlberg, C. (1996). Spotfire: an information exploration environment. *SIGMOD*, 25(4):25–29.

[Blei, 2012] Blei, D. M. (2012). Probabilistic topic models. *Communications of the ACM*, 55(4):77–84.

[Blei et al., 2003] Blei, D. M., Ng, A., and Jordan, M. (2003). Latent Dirichlet allocation. *JMLR*, 3.

[Chaney and Blei, 2012] Chaney, A. J.-B. and Blei, D. M. (2012). Visualizing topic models. In *ICWSM*.

[Chang et al., 2009] Chang, J., Boyd-Graber, J., Wang, C., Gerrish, S., and Blei, D. M. (2009). Reading tea leaves: How humans interpret topic models. In *NIPS*.

[Dou et al., 2011] Dou, W., Wang, X., Chang, R., and Ribarsky, W. (2011). ParallelTopics: A probabilistic approach to exploring document collections. In *VAST*.

[Eisenstein et al., 2012] Eisenstein, J., Chau, D. H., Kittur, A., and Xing, E. (2012). TopicViz: interactive topic exploration in document collections. In *CHI*.

[Hu et al., 2011] Hu, Y., Boyd-Graber, J., and Satinoff, B. (2011). Interactive topic modeling. In *ACL*.

[Nguyen et al., 2012] Nguyen, V.-A., Boyd-Graber, J., and Resnik, P. (2012). SITS: A hierarchical nonparametric model using speaker identity for topic segmentation in multiparty conversations. In *ACL*.

[North and Shneiderman, 2000] North, C. and Shneiderman, B. (2000). Snap-together visualization: a user interface for coordinating visualizations via relational schemata. In *AVI*, pages 128–135.

[Perer and Shneiderman, 2006] Perer, A. and Shneiderman, B. (2006). Balancing systematic and flexible exploration of social networks. *IEEE Transactions on Visualization and Computer Graphics*, 12(5):693–700.

[Purver, 2011] Purver, M. (2011). Topic segmentation. In *Spoken Language Understanding: Systems for Extracting Semantic Information from Speech*.

[Rogers and Norton, 2011] Rogers, T. and Norton, M. I. (2011). The artful dodger: Answering the wrong question the right way. *Journal of Experimental Psychology: Applied*, 17(2):139–147.

[Sopan et al., 2013] Sopan, A., Freier, M., Taieb-Maimon, M., Plaisant, C., Golbeck, J., and Shneiderman, B. (2013). Exploring data distributions: Visual design and evaluation. *JHCI*, 29(2):77–95.

[Wang Baldonado et al., 2000] Wang Baldonado, M. Q., Woodruff, A., and Kuchinsky, A. (2000). Guidelines for using multiple views in information visualization. In *AVI*, pages 110–119.

[Weaver, 2004] Weaver, C. (2004). Building highly-coordinated visualizations in Improvise. In *INFOVIS*.

Author Index